Geoff Tibballs is the [...] -
ing the bestselling [...]
Mammoth Book of D. [...] *ook*
of Comic Quotes, The [...] *vival Guide* and
Dad-isms. He has contributed to the *Ripley's Believe It
or Not!* annuals for more than twenty years. He lives in
Nottingham with his wife.

THE
GRUMPY
OLD
GITS'

JOKE BOOK

GEOFF TIBBALLS

G:

G:

First published in the UK in 2024
by Gemini Adult Books Ltd,
part of the Gemini Books Group

Based in Woodbridge and London

Marine House, Tide Mill Way,
Woodbridge, Suffolk, IP12 1AP
United Kingdom

www.geminibooks.com

Text © 2024 Gemini Books Group

Paperback ISBN 9781802471878
eBook ISBN 9781802472615

Design and typesetting by Danny Lyle

Printed in the UK
10 9 8 7 6 5 4 3 2 1

CONTENTS

INTRODUCTION

Prising a smile out of a grumpy old git can be as difficult – and painful – as extracting your own teeth. Unless they're talking about their grandchildren, when they suddenly remember how to beam with pride, a grumpy's natural expression is that of someone who has just been sucking a lemon. There's little appetite for merriment and frivolity. Instead they're too busy telling anyone who will listen how in their day household appliances were built to last for decades, you didn't have to drive for two hours to find the nearest bank branch, you had to possess a modicum of talent – other than one for self-promotion – to be considered a celebrity, cars were produced in a colour other than silver or black, and you didn't have to endure a twenty-minute wait, listen to repeated segments of Vivaldi's *The Four Seasons* and hear constant assurances that 'your call is important to us' before you could finally speak to customer services.

And when that diatribe is over, they will always manage to slip in the fact that, unlike the mollycoddled kids of today, they used to have to walk miles and miles to school every day, the distance becoming longer with each telling.

Grumpies can find fault with almost anything. The Grand Canyon is just 'a big hole in the ground', the Pyramids of Giza 'could do with some windows', and the ceiling of the Sistine Chapel 'should have been painted in white emulsion'. As for the Taj Mahal, 'too fancy by half', while the Great Wall of China would have 'looked better as a nice picket fence'.

Yet beneath that curmudgeonly exterior invariably lurks a heart of gold and a sharp, if reluctantly displayed, sense of humour. So you never know, this collection of senior-related jokes may even force that elusive smile. Just don't expect them to do it while anyone is around. That would ruin their reputation as a proud and fully paid-up member of the Grumpy Old Gits' Club.

1

HAVE I TOLD YOU ABOUT MY BAD BACK?

Having just turned sixty, George was eligible for an annual check-up at the local health centre. First, the nurse asked him how tall he was.

'I think I'm about five eleven,' said George.

She measured him and informed him that he was only five foot eight.

Next, she asked him if he knew how much he weighed.

'About 165 pounds,' said George.

She weighed him and the scale showed 186.

Then she took his blood pressure. 'It's very high,' she told him.

'Of course it's high,' he snapped. 'When I came in here I was tall and slim. Now I'm short and fat!'

* * *

A group of elderly people were discussing their various ailments. One said: 'My arthritis is so bad I can hardly grip this cup.'

Another said: 'My cataracts are so bad I can't even see to pour my coffee.'

Another said: 'I can't turn my head because of the constant throbbing pain in my neck.'

Another said: 'I get regular dizzy spells as a result of my low blood pressure.'

Another said: 'My sinusitis gives me blinding head-aches.'

Another said: 'I guess that's what happens when you get old.'

Another said: 'But we should be grateful that we can all still drive.'

* * *

Two senior citizens were enjoying a nice cup of tea and a biscuit. One said to the other: 'I'm really beginning to feel my age.'

'What makes you think that?' asked his friend. 'You seem quite sprightly to me.'

'Well, the other night my wife had gone up to bed early, so I was flicking through the various TV channels looking for something to watch and I stumbled across this adults-only channel. There was this lovely girl in a skimpy little French maid's outfit pushing a Hoover and bending over provocatively. And as her short skirt rode up, slightly exposing her pert little bottom and revealing just a hint of lacy panties, all I could think was: "We used to have a Hoover like that one."'

* * *

A man in his late seventies went to the doctor for a health check. A few days later, the doctor saw the old man walking down the street with a beautiful young woman on his arm.

The following day, the doctor bumped into him again. 'I saw you yesterday,' the doctor said, smiling. 'You seem to be doing well.'

'Just doing what you told me, doc,' said the old man. 'Get a hot mamma and be cheerful.'

'That's not what I said,' sighed the doctor. 'I said, "You've got a heart murmur – be careful."'

* * *

An old man went to the doctor, accompanied by his wife. As he was hard of hearing, he relied on her to relay the instructions of the medical staff.

'OK,' began the doctor. 'Will you take off your shirt please?'

'What did he say?' asked the old man.

'They want your shirt,' replied the wife.

So the old man took off his shirt, which was encrusted with dried-up food, and handed it to the nurse.

Next the doctor said to him: 'Would you please remove your socks so that I can examine your feet?'

'What did he say?' shouted the old man.

'They want your socks,' explained the wife.

As the old man was taking off his smelly socks, the nurse said: 'Also, sir, we need a stool sample and a urine sample.'

'What did she say?' boomed the old man. 'I couldn't hear a word.'

The wife said: 'They want your underpants.'

* * *

An elderly man went to see his doctor. 'You see, doc,' he explained, 'whenever I make love to my wife, I start to feel dizzy, my legs go weak and I find myself short of breath. I'm worried that it might be something serious.'

'Well,' said the doctor, 'it's not unusual to experience those symptoms during sex as you get older. Just remind me, how old are you?'

'Eighty-eight, doc.'

'And when did you first notice these symptoms?'

'Twice last night and twice again this morning.'

* * *

After suffering for weeks with a persistent cough, an old man decided to consult a pharmacist. The pharmacy assistant suggested a standard cough remedy, but, a week later, the old man returned to the shop to complain that the medicine was not working. So the assistant gave him a slightly stronger remedy in the hope that it would cure the cough. However a week later the old man returned again to complain that the latest recommended remedy was not working either. This time he saw the chief pharmacist.

A few days later, the chief pharmacist and his assistant happened to glance out of the window just as the old man was walking down the street. They couldn't help noticing that he was walking very slowly and deliberately but the good thing was that he didn't cough once.

'That's incredible,' said the assistant. 'He seems to be cured. What cough remedy did you give him?'

'I didn't give him a cough remedy,' replied the chief

pharmacist. 'I gave him a powerful laxative. Now he's afraid to cough!'

* * *

Two old ladies were sitting on a hard church pew during a long service. After a while, one whispered to the other: 'I think my bum is falling asleep.'

The other replied: 'I know. I've heard it snore three times already.'

* * *

A seventy-seven-year-old man had been left a widower following the death of his wife. He yearned for companionship and while walking in the park one afternoon he noticed an elegant, grey-haired lady sitting alone on a bench. Plucking up courage, he went over to her and asked whether she would mind if he sat with her. Looking up to see such a smartly-dressed gentleman, she readily agreed and shuffled along so that he could sit next to her.

For the next two hours the conversation between them flowed freely. They found they had many things in common – a love of film, literature and classical music and an appreciation of good food and fine wines. They even enjoyed travelling to the same parts of the world and both had always dreamed of owning a property in Tuscany. Furthermore, their spouses had died in the same year after long and happy marriages. Sensing that their connection was fate rather than mere coincidence, the old gentleman eventually turned to her and said: 'May I ask you two questions?'

'Of course,' she replied.

He then removed a handkerchief from his coat pocket and spread it on the ground in front of her. Very gingerly he got down on one knee and looked her tenderly in the eyes. 'Alice,' he began, 'I realise that we have only known each other for a couple of hours but we have so much in common that I feel I have known you all my life and that we are destined to be together. So would you do me the great honour of becoming my wife?'

She reached out for his hands and smiled: 'Yes, yes, a hundred times yes. I would be thrilled to marry you.' With that, she leaned over and kissed him sweetly on the cheek before adding: 'But you said you had two questions that you wanted to ask me. What is the second question?'

He held his back and grimaced: 'Will you help me get up?'

* * *

An elderly man rang the incontinence helpline and told the advisor: 'I have an incontinence problem. Before I go into details, is all the information I give you confidential?'

'Of course, sir,' said the advisor. 'Now, where are you ringing from?'

'The waist down.'

* * *

A merry widow celebrated her eightieth birthday on a luxurious Caribbean cruise. That evening she went to the bar, ordered a whisky with two drops of water and informed everyone present that today was her landmark birthday.

As she finished her drink, a fellow passenger insisted on buying her another.

'Thank you,' she said. 'I'll have another whisky with two drops of water please, bartender.'

When she had downed that, another passenger bought her a drink.

'How kind.' She smiled. 'I'll have another whisky with two drops of water please, bartender.'

When her glass was empty, the bartender decided to make her next drink on the house.

'That's very generous of you, young man,' she beamed. 'I'll have another whisky with two drops of water please.'

As he handed her the drink, the bartender said: 'One thing puzzles me, madam. Why do you always order your whisky with only two drops of water?'

She replied: 'When you're my age you've learned how to hold your alcohol, but holding your water is a different matter.'

* * *

On passing a hospital ward, a student nurse noticed an elderly man sitting on the side of the bed already dressed and with a suitcase at his feet. Aware that hospital regulations stipulated that any patient being discharged should use a wheelchair, she immediately fetched one for him.

'I don't need any help,' he protested.

'I'm sorry, sir, but rules are rules,' said the nurse. 'I must take you to the lift in a wheelchair.'

'Very well,' he sighed. 'If you insist.'

So she wheeled him to the lift. On the way down she asked him: 'Is your wife meeting you in reception?'

'I doubt it,' he replied. 'She's still upstairs in the bathroom changing out of her hospital gown!'

* * *

An elderly gentleman returned home from a doctor's appointment in a state of shock.

'What's the matter?' asked his wife.

'The doctor says I have only twenty-four hours to live.'

'Oh my!' she gasped. 'That's terrible. I don't know what to say. Is there anything I can do to make your remaining hours on earth as pleasant as possible?'

He thought about the offer for a moment and said: 'It would be nice to have sex one last time.'

'Of course.' She smiled, and they went to bed and made love.

Six hours later, he approached his wife again and said: 'Darling, I only have eighteen hours to live. Could we have sex one more time?'

'Why not?' she said, and they went to bed and made love once more.

That evening as they prepared for bed, he realised he had only ten hours to live. So he begged his wife for one more round of sex. She agreed, and they made love for a third time.

After that, she fell asleep but he was unable to settle. Eventually he looked at the bedside alarm clock and saw that he only had four hours to live. He tapped her on the shoulder and said: 'Darling, I only have another four hours. Do you think we could possibly have sex one final...'

At this, she sat bolt upright in bed and snapped: 'Listen, Albert, you don't have to get up in the morning, but I do!'

* * *

On waking up in bed one morning, a senior lady leaned over to give her husband an affectionate kiss.

'Keep away from me!' he yelled. 'I'm dead.'

'What are you taking about?' she said. 'We're both wide awake and talking. What on earth makes you think you're dead?'

'I must be dead,' he answered, 'because I woke up this morning and nothing hurts!'

* * *

A man in his sixties went to the doctor to seek advice on how to relieve his chronic constipation. 'It's terrible,' he said, 'I haven't been able to move my bowels in over a week.'

'I see,' said the doctor. 'Have you done anything about it?'

'Well, I sit on the toilet for at least half an hour in the morning and then again in the evening.'

'Sorry,' said the doctor, 'what I mean is, do you take anything?'

'Yes, I do,' said the patient. 'I take a good book.'

* * *

A retired gentleman visited the doctor for his six-monthly medical check-up. At the end of the examination, the doctor explained that the old man had a heart murmur.

'Do you smoke?' asked the doctor.

'No,' replied the old man. 'I gave up years ago.'

'Do you drink to excess?'

'No, I just enjoy the occasional glass of wine.'

'Do you mind me asking if you still have a sex life?'

'Yes, I still have a sex life.'

'Well,' sighed the doctor, 'I'm afraid that with your serious heart condition I would strongly advise you to give up half of your sex life.'

'Which half?' asked the old man. 'The looking or the thinking?'

* * *

Ahead of his first-ever night in a hospital, a grumpy old man began examining the bedside equipment. Playing with the bell cord that had been attached to his bed, he asked his son: 'What's this thing for?'

'It's a bell,' replied the son.

The old man pulled it several times. 'I can't hear it ringing,' he complained.

'No,' explained the son. 'It doesn't ring. It turns on a light in the hall for the nurse.'

The old man grumbled: 'If the nurse wants a light on in the hall, she can damn well turn it on herself!'

* * *

A sixty-year-old man informed his doctor that he could no longer help around the house like he used to. 'Ten years ago, I was able to wash a few dishes, even do a spot of ironing, but now it's all far too tiring.'

So the doctor examined him thoroughly. When the doctor had finished, the man said: 'Right, doc, tell me in plain English what is wrong with me.'

The doctor put down his stethoscope and said: 'There's nothing wrong with you. In plain English you're lazy.'

'OK,' said the man, 'now give me the medical term so I can tell my wife.'

* * *

An elderly couple were attending church one Sunday when, part-way through the service, the wife leaned over and whispered to her husband: 'I've just let out a silent fart. What do you think I should do?'

The husband replied: 'Put a new battery in your hearing aid.'

* * *

An old man attended a school reunion but was dismayed to find that his surviving classmates only wanted to talk about their various ailments – heart conditions, kidney stones, liver problems. When he got home, his wife asked him how the evening had gone.

'It wasn't much of a reunion,' he groaned. 'It was more like an organ recital.'

* * *

A little old lady boarded a Greyhound bus in New Orleans. Ten minutes into the journey, she tottered up to the front of the bus and asked the driver: 'Are we in Houston yet?'

'No, ma'am,' replied the driver politely. 'We're not in Houston yet. We've only just left New Orleans. But don't worry, I'll tell you when we get to Houston.'

Twenty minutes later, she again tottered up to the front of the bus and asked the driver: 'Are we in Houston yet?'

'No, ma'am,' said the driver, struggling to contain his irritation. 'Like I said, I'll let you know when we are.'

Twenty minutes later, she once more tottered up to the front of the bus and asked the driver: 'Are we in Houston yet?'

'No, we're not,' he said sharply. 'Like I say, I'll tell you when we are.'

She kept this up for the next five hours. Every twenty minutes, she would totter up to the front of the bus and ask the driver if they had reached Houston yet. And each time he would reply with a simple but firm 'no', and she would return to her seat. It reached the stage where he was constantly glancing at his watch in anticipation of her question. His palms and brow were sweating, his nerves were in tatters. So it came as a huge relief when Houston bus station finally came into view and he was able to announce: 'OK, madam, *this* is Houston. Off you get.'

'Oh no, driver,' she said. 'I'm going all the way to Los Angeles. It's just that my son told me that when I got to Houston I should take my blood pressure tablet.'

* * *

An elderly man who was seriously overweight was standing on the bathroom scales. Thinking that he was holding in his stomach in a desperate attempt to reduce his weight, his wife remarked: 'I don't think that will help.'

'It will,' he said. 'It's the only way I can read the numbers!'

* * *

Two medical students were strolling through the park when they noticed an elderly man tottering along awkwardly with his legs wide apart. The first student said to the other: 'I bet that old man has Von Hyseghem syndrome. That's exactly how people with that condition walk.'

The second student disagreed. 'No, I think he has Mecklenberg syndrome. Remember, we learned about it in class last year. To my mind, that old man's strange gait displays all the classic symptoms.'

To resolve the dispute, they decided to approach the old man and ask him in person. 'Excuse me,' they said, 'we're medical students and we couldn't help noticing the distinctive way you walk with your legs wide apart. But we can't agree on what condition you have. Could you enlighten us, please?'

The old man said: 'I will tell you, but first I want to hear what you think it is.'

The first student said: 'I think it's Von Hyseghem syndrome.'

The old man said: 'You thought, but you are wrong.'

The second student said: 'I think it's Mecklenberg syndrome.'

The old man said: 'You thought, but you are wrong.'

'So what do you have?' they asked.

The old man replied: 'I thought it was wind, but I was wrong.'

* * *

Recovering from a serious illness, an elderly lady begged her doctor: 'Please keep me alive for another three months so that I can attend my grandson's wedding.'

'We'll do our best,' said the doctor.

The doctor was as good as his word and the old lady was able to attend her grandson's wedding, for which she was extremely grateful.

A couple of months after the ceremony, she again went to see the doctor. 'My grandson's wife is pregnant,' she explained, 'so please can you keep me alive for another seven months so that I can welcome the birth of my first great-grandchild?'

'We'll certainly try,' said the doctor, and indeed the old lady was still alive when the baby was born.

Several years passed and the old lady managed to defy the odds to celebrate her ninetieth birthday. The following week, she called on her doctor once more: 'Doctor,' she began, 'do you remember how you helped me live long enough to see my grandson get married?'

'Yes, I do.'

'And later how you made sure I was still around for the birth of my great-grandchild?'

'Yes, I do.'

'Well, I have another favour to ask. As you know, I've just celebrated my ninetieth birthday. And I just purchased a new mattress.'

'Yes?'

'It has a fifteen-year guarantee...'

* * *

A sixty-five-year-old man needed a pacemaker, but the National Health Service waiting list was so long that he elected to go private instead. So he visited an eminent surgeon who said that he was perfectly willing to fit a pacemaker but warned that it would cost fifteen thousand pounds.

'I didn't realise it would be that expensive,' said the patient, scratching his head. 'But I have an idea. I know someone who is brilliant with gadgets and electronics. If I provide my own pacemaker with help from him, will you carry out the implant for me?'

'It's a little irregular,' said the surgeon, 'but if you're confident in the abilities of this friend of yours I don't see why not.'

A few weeks later, the patient returned to the surgeon with the pacemaker. The surgeon duly implanted the device in his chest, wired him up and sent him on his way.

Three months later, the patient returned for a check-up.

'Any problems at all?' asked the surgeon.

'Only one,' said the patient. 'Every time I get an erection, the garage door opens!'

* * *

A senior man loved baked beans even though they gave him the most terrible wind. But because it was his birthday he decided to treat himself and on his way home he stopped at a café for a triple portion of beans on toast. As he emerged from the café, he was confident that he could get rid of all the wind on the fifteen-minute walk home.

He walked through the front door of his house, buttocks firmly clenched, to find his wife waiting for him. 'I've got a birthday surprise for you,' she said. Before he could say anything, she put a blindfold on him, led him to his chair at the head of the dinner table and made him promise not to look. Just then the phone rang, and she went into the hallway to answer it.

Sat on the chair, he could no longer contain his wind. He could hear his wife's voice in the hallway, so he felt it was safe to release one or two little farts. Leaning first one way and then the other, he allowed nature to take its course, but instead of a few silent puffs of air, they came out to the sound of machine-gun fire. And the stench was horrendous – so noxious that even he started to feel faint. He desperately tried to wave the smell away with his hands in the hope that it would have gone by the time his wife returned.

Finally she came back into the room, removed his blindfold and said: 'Surprise!'

He opened his eyes to see a dozen guests seated around the table.

* * *

Waking up in the hospital recovery room following surgery, an elderly man sighed: 'Thank goodness that's over.'

'You're lucky,' said the guy in the next bed. 'They left a scalpel inside me and had to cut me open again.'

'That's awful!' said the old man.

'They had to open me up again too,' said the guy in the bed on the other side. 'To find their sponge.'

'How terrible!' said the old man.

Just then, the surgeon who had operated on the old man poked his head around the door and asked: 'Has anyone seen my hat?'

The old man fainted.

* * *

In a gesture of support, a woman accompanied her elderly husband to the doctor's for his regular health check. Afterwards, the doctor took her to one side and solemnly informed her: 'I'm afraid it doesn't look good for your husband. Unless you adhere to a strict routine, he will probably be dead in six months. This is what you must do. Every morning you must carefully prepare a healthy breakfast for him – cereal, fruit and a slice of toast. And in the evening you must cook him a nutritious meal. He must not undertake any strenuous activities around the house and that includes vacuuming, cleaning the windows, carrying the shopping and doing the ironing. You need to wait on him hand and foot. I understand that this will mean extra work for you but it really is the only way to keep him alive.'

On their way home, the husband asked his wife what the doctor had said.

'Oh, that,' she answered. 'He said you'll be dead in six months.'

* * *

An elderly gentleman phoned the hospital one day and asked: 'Is it possible to speak to someone who can tell me how a patient is doing?'

'Certainly, sir,' replied the operator. 'What's the patient's name and ward number?'

'George Spencer on Ward Fifteen.'

'Thank you. Let me put you on hold while I check with the ward nurse.'

A couple of minutes later, the operator returned to the phone. 'Hello, sir, it's good news. George is doing very well. His blood tests have come back fine and the consultant is hoping to discharge him tomorrow.'

'Thank you very much. I have been so worried. That is good news.'

'You're welcome,' said the operator. 'Is George your son?'

'No,' said the old man. 'I'm George Spencer on Ward Fifteen. Nobody ever tells me anything.'

* * *

A recent retiree asked his doctor if he thought he would live to the age of one hundred.

The doctor asked him: 'Do you smoke?'

'No,' replied the man. 'I've never smoked.'

'Do you drink alcohol?'

'No, I've never touched a drop of alcohol in my life.'

'Do you gamble, drive fast cars and fool around with women?'

'No, I've never done any of those things either.'

'Well then,' said the doctor, 'why would you want to live to be a hundred?'

* * *

An elderly man booked an appointment with his doctor for advice on how to deal with his chronic constipation. The doctor asked him about his diet, and the old man admitted that the only vegetable he ever ate was peas.

'That's probably the reason you're always feeling constipated,' said the doctor. 'All those peas you've been eating over the years have clogged up your system. I'm sorry, but you'll have to give them up.'

Several years later, the old man was sitting in the lounge of a retirement home chatting to two of the female residents. The conversation turned to food and drink. One of the ladies said: 'If there's one thing I miss in life, it's a nice rasher of crispy bacon. But I had to stop eating it for health reasons.'

The other lady said: 'It's the same with me and cheese. I adore soft cheese, but the doctor told me it was making my cholesterol too high, so I had to stop buying it.'

'I know what you mean,' said the old man. 'I haven't had a pea for nine years.'

The two ladies immediately leaped to their feet and screamed: 'Right, anyone who can't swim, grab a table!'

* * *

A man in his late eighties was undergoing his regular health check at the medical centre.

'How are you today?' asked the doctor.

The old man grinned from ear to ear. 'Hey, doc, I've only gone and got a twenty-year-old girl pregnant! Not bad at my age, eh? I bet you didn't think I still had it in me. And she wants us to get married next month.'

The doctor thought for a moment and said: 'Let me tell you a story. I knew a man who was a keen hunter, but one day he left home in a hurry and accidentally picked up his umbrella instead of his shotgun. Later that day, he came face to face with a huge grizzly bear. The hunter raised his umbrella, pointed it at the bear and squeezed the handle. And guess what, the bear dropped dead on the spot.'

'That's impossible,' said the old man. 'Someone else must have shot that bear.'

The doctor said: 'That's kind of what I'm getting at...'

* * *

A pensioner had his first appointment with a new doctor. The doctor immediately noticed that the patient had very red cheeks.

'It's high blood pressure, doctor. It comes from my family.'

'Your mother's side or your father's side?' queried the doctor.

'Neither. It's from my wife's family.'

The doctor scratched his head. 'I'm fairly sure that's not medically possible. I really don't think you can get high blood pressure from your *wife*'s family.'

The old man said: 'You should try spending a weekend with them!'

* * *

Keen to get fit, a man phoned his local gym and said: 'I'm seventy years old and I want you to teach me how to do the splits.'

The gym assistant asked: 'How flexible are you?'

The man said: 'I can't make Tuesdays or Fridays.'

* * *

An elderly lady called the medical helpline and said: 'Please help me. My husband fell asleep with his mouth wide open and he's swallowed a mouse. What shall I do?'

'Don't worry,' said the helpline operator. 'All you need to do is tie a piece of cheese to a length of string and lower it into your husband's mouth. As soon as the mouse starts nibbling at the cheese, pull the string out and the mouse will come too.'

'Thank you so much,' said the old lady. 'I'll go straight round to the fishmonger's and buy a cod's head.'

'Why do you want a cod's head?' asked the operator.

'Oh, I forgot to tell you,' said the old lady. 'I've got to get the cat out first!'

* * *

A senior couple went to the doctor for their annual physicals. The man went in first and after he was finished the doctor sent him back out to the waiting room and called in the wife.

The doctor said earnestly: 'Before I examine you, I have to tell you that I'm a little concerned about your husband. I asked him how he was feeling and he said he had never felt better. He told me that when he got up this morning he went to the bathroom, opened the door and God turned the light on for him. And when he was done, he shut the door and God turned the light out for him.'

'The silly old fool!' exclaimed the wife. 'He's been peeing in the fridge again.'

* * *

An old man was all but deaf until he was finally given a new hearing aid that allowed him to hear perfectly for the first time in years. Monitoring his patient's progress, his doctor said: 'Your family must be really pleased that you can hear again.'

'I haven't told them yet,' admitted the old man. 'I just sit around and listen to their conversations. I've changed my will three times in the last month!'

* * *

Three men were talking about their respective health problems.

The seventy-year-old said: 'My problem is I wake up every morning at seven and it takes me at least twenty minutes to pee.'

The eighty-year-old said: 'My problem is I wake up at eight and it takes me at least half an hour to have a bowel movement.'

The ninety-year-old said: 'At seven I always pee like a horse and at eight I crap like a cow.'

'So what's your problem?' asked the other two.

'I don't wake up till nine!'

2

LIFE CAN BE SO CONFUSING

Over a morning coffee, three old ladies were sitting at the kitchen table discussing the difficulties of ageing.

The first lady said: 'I'm afraid that I'm becoming extremely forgetful. This morning I went into the spare bedroom and I couldn't remember for the life of me what I was looking for.'

'That's nothing,' said the second lady. 'The other day I was standing at the foot of the stairs and I couldn't remember whether I was about to go up or if I had just come down.'

'I'm happy to say that my memory is as good as ever, touch wood,' said the third lady, rapping her knuckles on the table. 'That must be the door – I'll get it.'

* * *

A widowed couple in their eighties had been dating for more than five years when, sensing that time might soon be running out for both of them, he finally asked her to marry him. Without hesitation, she said 'yes.'

However, by the following morning, he couldn't remember her reply. Had she accepted or declined his offer of marriage? In desperation he tried to visualise her face. Was she smiling when he got down on one knee because she was happy at the thought of the forthcoming proposal or was she gently preparing him for rejection? Eventually he concluded that the only way to solve the problem was to phone her.

'I am so embarrassed to have to admit this,' he told her hesitantly, 'but when I proposed to you yesterday, did you say "yes" or "no"?'

'Thank goodness you called,' she replied. 'I remember saying "yes" to someone yesterday, but I couldn't remember who it was!'

* * *

Three retired men were playing golf. Each of them struggled with their hearing. Halfway round the course, the first old man said to the second: 'Windy, isn't it?'

'No,' replied the second. 'It's Thursday.'

At which point the third old man said: 'So am I. Let's have a beer.'

* * *

A senior couple stopped at a roadside restaurant for lunch while driving to the coast. After returning to the car, they had driven for about twenty minutes on their onward journey when the woman suddenly remembered that she had left her glasses in the restaurant.

Her husband complained bitterly about having to stop the car, turn around and drive all the way back to the restaurant. 'How could you be so forgetful as to leave your glasses behind?' he grumbled. 'At this rate by the time we get to the coast it will be time to head back home again! I really could do without all this.'

He was still moaning when they pulled up again outside the restaurant. As his wife climbed out of the car, he leaned over and said: 'And while you're in there, you may as well get my hat.'

* * *

An eighty-eight-year-old man was sitting on a park bench sobbing. Seeing his distress, a teenage boy asked him what the problem was.

'I'm madly in love with a twenty-one-year-old girl,' wailed the old man. 'She is stunningly beautiful, kind, considerate, a fantastic cook and we have the most amazing sex twice a day.'

'So why are you crying?' said the boy.
'I can't remember where we live!'

* * *

An elderly woman who was hard of hearing went to the doctor to find out whether there was any risk of her getting pregnant again at her time of life.

The doctor told her: 'Mrs Jameson, you're seventy-five, and although one can never rule out an act of God, for you to have a baby it would be a miracle.'

When she returned home, her husband asked her what the doctor had said.

'I didn't quite catch it all,' she admitted, 'but it sounded a bit fishy. Something about an act of cod, and if I had a baby it would be a mackerel.'

* * *

While passing the bank one morning, a man decided to go inside and open a new savings account. The clerk fetched the relevant form and asked him for his age.

The old man looked back with a glazed expression and said: 'I'm terribly sorry. My mind has gone blank. I've completely forgotten how old I am. If you give me a couple of minutes, it will come to me.'

He then began counting on his fingers and eventually announced triumphantly: 'Eighty-three!'

'Thank you,' said the clerk. 'And could I have your name, please?'

Once again the old man looked bewildered, but then he started singing quietly to himself, his head bobbing from side to side. After about thirty seconds, he replied: 'Ah, that's it. Michael.'

The clerk was intrigued by the old man's memory aids and said: 'I hope you don't mind me asking, sir, but what were you doing when I asked you what your name was? You appeared to be singing to yourself.'

'I was,' replied the old man. 'I was running through that song. You know the one. "Happy birthday to you, happy birthday to you, happy birthday dear..."'

* * *

An elderly couple were struggling to remember everyday things, so, on the advice of their doctor, they reluctantly agreed to write everything down in future.

One evening they were watching TV when the husband got up from his chair.

'Where are you going?' asked his wife.

'To the kitchen,' he replied.

'Will you get me a bowl of ice cream while you're there?'

'Sure,' he said.

'Don't you think you should write it down so you don't forget it?'

'No need,' he said confidently. 'I'm sure I can remember that.'

'Well, I would also like some strawberries on top,' continued the wife. 'You ought to write that down because I know you'll forget them otherwise.'

'I can remember that,' he insisted. 'You want a bowl of ice cream with strawberries. Simple.'

She then said: 'Actually I would also like whipped cream on top of the strawberries. You'd better write that down because you're sure to forget that.'

'I don't need to write it down,' he said tetchily. 'I can remember it.'

Twenty minutes later, he returned from the kitchen and handed her a plate of bacon and eggs.

She stared at the plate for a moment in disbelief and said: 'You forgot my toast!'

* * *

A man in his seventies was seriously overweight, so his doctor placed him on a strict diet, telling him:

'I want you to eat regularly for two days, then skip a day, and repeat that pattern for two weeks. By the time I next see you, you should have lost five pounds.'

When the patient returned two weeks later, the doctor was amazed to discover that he had lost just over twenty pounds. 'That's really impressive,' said the doctor. 'Did you follow my instructions?'

'Yes,' said the patient, 'but I was afraid I was going to drop dead on the third day.'

'What, from hunger?'

'No, from skipping.'

* * *

An elderly guest phoned hotel reception to complain that he was trapped in his room.

'I can't get out,' he said.

'Why not?' asked the receptionist. 'Have you tried the door?'

'Of course I have,' said the guest. 'I'm not daft. But there are only three doors in here. The first is the bathroom, the second is the wardrobe, and the third has a sign on it saying "Do Not Disturb".'

* * *

Three men in their eighties had volunteered to take part in a cognitive test at their local health centre. The doctor in charge began by asking the first man: 'What is two times two?'

'319,' he replied.

The doctor wrote down the answer and then asked the second man: 'What is two times two?'

'October,' came the reply.

'I see,' said the doctor, making a note of the answer.

The doctor then turned to the third man and asked: 'What is two times two?'

'Four,' he replied.

'Very good,' said the doctor. 'How did you reach that answer?'

'It was easy,' said the third old man. 'I simply subtracted 319 from October.'

* * *

A little girl was puzzled why her grandfather had three pairs of glasses. He explained: 'I have one pair for distance, one for reading, and the third pair to look for the other two.'

* * *

Two friends, Ruth and Elizabeth, had enjoyed a weekly lunch at a local restaurant for more than forty years. But, as the years passed, Ruth began to feel that they should be talking about more important matters than their usual discussions about the weather, TV, and soft furnishings. 'Next time,' she suggested, 'instead of talking about what colour tiles you're going to have in your new bathroom, why don't we debate world affairs?'

'Fine,' said Elizabeth. 'If that's what you want.'

So the following week, after they had ordered their starter, Elizabeth said: 'Go on then, Ruth. You start the serious political debate.'

'Very well,' said Ruth. 'What do you think about Red China?'

'Only one thing,' replied Elizabeth. 'It won't go with your brown tablecloth.'

* * *

Maurice was becoming increasingly worried that his wife might have a hearing problem. So while they sat in their favourite armchairs watching TV one evening, he called across the room to her.

'Can you hear me, Joyce?' he asked.

Silence.

Thirty seconds later, he tried again a little louder. 'Can you hear me, Joyce?'

Silence.

So he tried for a third time, almost shouting: 'Can you hear me, Joyce?'

She snapped back: 'For the third time, yes!'

* * *

Three friends found that the older they got, the more confused they tended to become. One day the three were chatting away happily on the platform at their local train station, but were so engrossed in their conversation that they didn't hear the guard blow his whistle to signal the train's impending departure. As the train started to pull away, two of the men just about managed to climb aboard, but the third didn't make it.

With the train disappearing into the distance, the guard strolled over to console the stranded passenger. 'Never mind,' said the guard. 'Two of you made it and there's another train in an hour.'

'No, you don't understand,' said the man. 'They came to see *me* off!'

* * *

An elderly man was driving along the highway when he received a frantic phone call from his wife. She told him: 'George, please be careful. I just heard on the news that there's a crazy driver on Route 55 driving the wrong way!'

'Honey, I hate to worry you,' said George, 'but it's even worse than what they're reporting. I'm on Route 55 and they're *all* driving the wrong way!'

* * *

A senior couple sat down to breakfast and listened to the weather report on the radio. The announcer said: 'There will be six inches of snow today, and a local emergency has been declared. You must park your car on the odd-numbered side of the street.'

'What a pain!' sighed the husband, abandoning his coffee, 'but I guess I must do what they say.'

The next morning at breakfast, the radio announcer issued another weather warning. 'Today there will be eight inches of snow, so another local emergency has been declared. Please park your car on the even-numbered side of the street.'

Again the husband sighed, got up from the table and complied with the emergency order.

On the third morning at breakfast, the radio announcer declared ominously: 'Today there will be twelve inches of snow, and another local emergency has been declared. You must park your car...'

Just then, there was a power cut, so the couple were unable to hear the rest of the announcement. 'What lousy timing!' exclaimed the husband in a worried tone. 'What am I going to do now?'

'I'm not sure,' replied his wife. 'Maybe you should just leave the car in the garage today.'

* * *

Two old men were sitting down to breakfast. One said: 'Do you know you've got a suppository in your left ear?'

'Really?' said the other. 'I'm glad you told me. Now I think I know where I put my hearing aid.'

* * *

Two elderly ladies who had known each other for a long time were sitting outside a coffee shop. Suddenly one looked at the other with a blank expression and said: 'I don't know how to say this. We've been friends for years and years, but, all of a sudden,

I can't remember your name. I've been through every letter of the alphabet in the hope that it would jog my memory but it hasn't worked. I simply can't remember it. I'm so sorry. What is your name?'

Her friend stared back at her in silence for the best part of two minutes before saying: 'How soon do you need to know?'

* * *

John trudged home after a round of golf to be greeted by his wife.

'How did you get on?' she asked.

'OK, I guess,' he sighed. 'I can still hit the ball pretty well, but my eyesight has become so bad that I can't always see where it goes. I've lost nine balls just in the past week.'

'Perhaps it's time for you to face facts, darling,' she said, smiling. 'You're seventy-three now and your vision won't be as good as it once was. Why don't you take my brother Tom along next time?

'But Tom's over eighty and doesn't even play any more.'

'I know, but he does have excellent eyesight and could watch your ball for you.'

So John agreed to take Tom along to his next game. At the first hole, John sent his tee shot soaring into the distance. 'Did you see where it went?' he asked Tom.

'I certainly did,' said Tom.

'Well, where is it?' said John as they began to set off in pursuit.

'I forget.'

* * *

An old woman from the country was visiting the big city for the first time in her life. Having lived on a remote ranch for over seventy years, she was a little apprehensive about whether she would manage to cope with all the hustle, bustle and sophistication. Anxious not to show herself up, she checked in at a smart hotel and let the bellboy take her bags from the foyer. She quickly followed him but as the door closed, her face fell.

'Young man,' she raged. 'I may be old and not used to city life, but I'm not stupid. I paid good money and this room won't do at all. It's way short of what I expected. It's small and poky, there's no window and no furniture. Hell, there's not even a bed!'

'Madam,' replied the bellboy calmly, 'this isn't your room. It's the lift.'

* * *

Two senior ladies, Rosemary and Dorothy, went to visit their friend Gloria. The three ladies had been sitting chatting for a while when Gloria suddenly rose to her feet and said: 'How forgetful of me! You have been here nearly an hour and I haven't offered you coffee.'

So Gloria went to the kitchen, made some coffee and returned with three cups.

Forty minutes later, Gloria suddenly got up again and declared: 'How forgetful of me! You've been here all this time and I haven't even offered you coffee.'

So again she went to the kitchen, made some coffee and returned with three cups.

Half an hour later, Gloria suddenly jumped up once more, saying: 'How forgetful of me! You've been here for over two hours and I haven't even offered you coffee.'

Once more, she went to the kitchen, made some coffee and returned with three cups.

Finally it was time for the two guests to leave. After saying their goodbyes to Gloria, Rosemary turned to Dorothy and said, 'Don't you think Gloria was behaving a bit strangely? All that time we spent there and she didn't even offer us coffee!'

Dorothy looked at her in amazement. 'What?! You've been to see Gloria? Why didn't you tell me?'

* * *

A police officer stopped a car on a quiet country road and walked over to the elderly driver. 'Excuse me, ma'am,' he said, 'but I've been following you for two miles and you've been weaving all over the road. Is there an explanation for your erratic driving?'

'Thank goodness you're here, officer,' she gasped. 'I nearly had an accident. I looked up and there was a tree directly in front of me. I swerved to the left and there was another tree. So I swerved to the right and there was another tree. It was absolutely terrifying.'

The officer calmly reached over to the rear view mirror and said: 'Ma'am, there was no tree. It was your air freshener.'

* * *

An elderly lady tried to phone her local bank branch but instead she was put through to the bank's call centre in Asia.

'Is that the High Street branch?' she asked.

'No, madam,' explained the voice at the other end of the line. 'It is now company policy to deal with customer phone calls centrally.'

'But I really need to speak to the branch,' said the old lady.

'Madam, if you just tell me your reason for calling the bank I am certain I can be of help to you.'

'I don't think you can, young man,' the old lady persisted. 'I need to speak to the branch.'

The call centre operator was equally emphatic. 'Madam, there is nothing that the branch can help you with that cannot be dealt with by me.'

'Very well then,' sighed the old lady. 'Can you check whether I left my gloves on the bank counter when I came in this morning?'

* * *

An ageing husband never referred to his wife by her real name. Instead, he always called her pet names like Sugar Lump, Kitten, and Honey Bunch. His friend thought it was sweet and remarked: 'I really like how you call her those endearing names. It shows how much you love her.'

'To tell the truth,' said the husband, 'I forgot her real name years ago.'

* * *

An elderly man went into a hardware store and asked for a chainsaw that was capable of cutting down half a dozen trees in under an hour. The sales assistant persuaded him to spend two hundred and fifty pounds on a state-of-the art model, which he promised would do the job perfectly.

But the next day the old man returned to the shop, placed the chainsaw on the counter and angrily informed the assistant: 'This expensive chainsaw you sold me is useless! It took me the whole day to cut down just one tree!'

'I don't understand,' said the assistant. 'This model has excellent reviews.'

With that, the assistant picked up the chainsaw and started it up to see what the problem was.

The old man said: 'What's that noise?'

* * *

Two elderly ladies, Ethel and Sybil, went for an after-noon drive in a huge four-by-four vehicle. Both women were so tiny that they could only just see over the dashboard, and when they came to a junction they sped straight through even though the light was red.

The incident troubled Ethel, who was sitting in the passenger seat. She thought to herself: 'Maybe I'm imagining it but I swear we just went through a red light.'

A couple of minutes later, they sailed through another red light. Ethel was becoming increasingly anxious but still refrained from saying anything.

Moments later, they went through a third red light, avoiding a collision by inches and prompting a cacophony of angry car horns. This near miss finally stirred Ethel into speaking. 'Sybil,' she said, her voice trembling, 'Do you realise you've just driven through three red lights? You could have got us killed!'

'Oh,' said Sybil, 'am I driving?'

* * *

Two senior men were talking about cars. One admitted that he always left his car keys in the ignition.

'You shouldn't do that,' said the other.

'But if I take them out of the ignition, I can never find them again.'

'That's all very well, but what happens if someone steals your car?'

'That wouldn't be a problem. I always keep a spare set of keys in the glove compartment.'

* * *

An elderly widower enjoyed going to the theatre and would watch several plays at different venues every month. On one occasion, an usher found him crawling on his hands and knees beneath the seats in the stalls during the first act of a serious drama.

'Sir, what are you doing?' hissed the usher. 'You're disturbing everyone around you.'

'I've lost my gum,' replied the old man as he continued to search under the seats.

'Is that all?' said the usher in astonishment. 'Please, let me offer you a fresh stick of gum so that you can return to your seat and watch the rest of the play in peace. A stick of gum is not worth all the nuisance you're causing.'

'You don't understand,' said the old man. 'My false teeth are in that gum!'

* * *

An old gentleman was sitting alone in an up-market bar, nursing a gin and tonic. Suddenly his attention was caught by the arrival of an attractive lady of similar vintage. Ascertaining that she, too, was alone, he slowly levered himself up from his seat, tottered over to the bar, sat down next to her and said: 'Tell me, do I come here often?'

* * *

An elderly man called the police to report that his car had been broken into. 'Those thieving little layabouts have taken everything,' he wailed, 'the stereo, the steering wheel, the handbrake, the clutch, and even the accelerator.'

The police operator asked him to keep calm and told him that an officer was on his way.

A few minutes later, the officer radioed in an update. 'There was no break-in. He got into the back seat by mistake.'

* * *

A retired couple went to another couple's house for dinner. Afterwards, while the women disappeared into the kitchen, the two men finished the bottle of wine at the table in the dining room. The conversation turned to food and one of the men began waxing lyrical about a restaurant that he and his wife had been to for their golden wedding anniversary. 'It was the most amazing place,' he gushed, 'and the food was delicious.'

'Sounds great,' said the other man. 'What was the name of the restaurant?'

'Oh, that's so frustrating. I can't remember the name. I hate it when that happens. Um, what's that flower that smells nice and has thorns?'

'A rose?'

'That's it,' he said triumphantly before turning to the kitchen and calling out: 'Hey, Rose, what was the name of the restaurant we went to for our golden wedding anniversary?'

* * *

Following a shopping expedition to her local supermarket, an elderly lady forgot where she had parked her car. Noticing that she was becoming increasingly agitated, the store security officer asked if he could be of assistance.

'I can't find my car,' she said.

'What make is it?' he asked.

She looked at him blankly and said: 'Name some.'

* * *

A group of seventeen-year-old college girls decided to meet up for dinner to mark the end of exams. After debating where best to eat, they decided on Gianni's Bar because the food was cheap and the cutest boy in class lived around the corner.

Ten years later, the same girlfriends – now aged twenty-seven – discussed where to meet up for dinner. Eventually they settled on Gianni's Bar because the beer was cheap, the band was good and there were always plenty of good-looking men there.

Ten years later, the same girlfriends – now thirty-seven – discussed where to meet for dinner. Finally they agreed on Gianni's Bar because it served decent wine, it was near the gym and if they got there after eight there would be no children running around.

Ten years later, the same girlfriends – now forty-seven – discussed where to go for dinner. Finally they agreed on Gianni's Bar because the cocktail menu was extensive and the waiters wore tight jeans.

Ten years later, the same girlfriends – now fifty-seven – discussed where to meet for dinner. Finally they agreed on Gianni's Bar because the air-conditioning worked well and the vegetarian options on the menu were good for their cholesterol.

Ten years later, the same girlfriends – now sixty-seven – discussed where to meet for dinner. Eventually they chose Gianni's Bar because the lighting was good, the menu was in large print and they could get special seniors' rates if they went early.

Ten years later, the same girlfriends – now seventy-seven – debated where to meet up for dinner. After lengthy consultation, they agreed on Gianni's Bar because it had wheelchair access and the food wasn't too hot and spicy.

Ten years later, the same girlfriends – now eighty-seven – discussed where to go for dinner. Eventually they agreed on Gianni's Bar because they had never been there before.

3

IT'S ALL TOO MUCH EFFORT AT MY AGE

A senior lady went to the doctor to see if there was anything he could recommend to renew her husband's interest in sex. She explained that they hadn't made love for more than seven years because all he wanted to do in bed was read a book.

'Well,' said the doctor. 'What about Viagra? That should increase his libido.'

'Doctor,' she sighed, 'I can't even get him to take an aspirin when he has a headache.'

The doctor had an idea. 'Perhaps if you crushed the Viagra into a powder, you could stir it into his coffee and that way he would never know.'

'That sounds a good plan,' she agreed. 'I'll definitely try it.'

Two weeks later, she returned to the doctor's.

'How did it go?' he asked.

'Terrible, just terrible,' she said.

'Did the crushed Viagra in his coffee not work?'

'Oh yes, it worked alright. He ripped off his clothes there and then and we made passionate love on the table. It was the best sex I'd had in years.'

'Then what's the problem?' asked the doctor.

'I'll never be able to show my face in that restaurant again!'

* * *

A newly-wed couple in their seventies booked an appointment with a fertility expert to determine whether it was still possible at their age for them to produce a child. The consultant told them that recent scientific advances had significantly improved their chances, but before he could give a definitive answer he would need the husband to submit a semen sample. So he gave them a jar to take home and asked them to return once they had got a sample.

Three days later, the couple went back to the consultant with an empty jar.

'Oh,' said the consultant. 'What went wrong?'

'I'm so sorry,' said the husband. 'First I tried my right hand and then I tried my left hand. My wife tried her right hand and then she tried her left hand. She even took her teeth out and used her mouth. But no matter how hard we tried we still couldn't get the lid off that damn jar!'

* * *

An elderly gentleman went to the pharmacy and asked the pharmacist for some Viagra.

'How many do you want?' asked the pharmacist.

'Only a few because I cut each tablet into four pieces,' said the old man.

'A quarter of a Viagra tablet is too small a dose,' said the pharmacist. 'That won't enable you to have intercourse.'

'Listen, I'm eighty-eight years old. I'm way past even thinking about sex. I just want it to stick out far enough so I don't pee on my shoes.'

* * *

A woman took her elderly husband by the hand and whispered in his ear: 'Tonight I'm going to give you super sex.'

'Sounds great,' he replied. 'I'll have the soup.'

* * *

Two elderly widows, Maud and Hermione, were chatting over coffee. Maud confided: 'Next week I'm going on a date with Ivor Richardson from the lunch club.'

Hermione raised her eyebrows. 'Are you indeed? Well, let me tell you I went out with him last month and it was quite an evening. He turned up at my apartment immaculately dressed and carrying a lovely bouquet of flowers for me. He then ordered a limousine to take me to the best restaurant in town where we shared a bottle of Dom Perignon and afterwards we went to see a show. He was a perfect gentlemen until we got back to my apartment where he suddenly turned into a wild animal. He ripped off my expensive new dress and had vigorous sex with me twice over the ottoman.'

'Oh, my!' said Maud. 'Do you think I should cancel our date?'

'Goodness, no,' replied Hermione. 'I'm just saying wear an old dress.'

* * *

An old man sat down in the confessional booth at his local church and said: 'Forgive me, Father, for I have sinned.'

'Tell me about your sins,' said the priest.

'Well, Father, I'm eighty-nine-years-old, I've been married for over sixty years and we have five lovely children and twelve grandchildren. I've never strayed before but last night I made love to two beautiful nineteen-year-old girls. And we did it three times.'

'I see,' said the priest. 'And when was the last time you were in confession?'

'I've never been to confession, Father,' said the old man. 'I'm Jewish.'

'So why are you telling me?' asked the priest.

'I'm telling everyone!'

* * *

A senior couple were sitting quietly on the porch in their rocking chairs when, without warning, the husband suddenly leaned over and prodded his wife in the arm.

'What was that for?' she demanded to know.

'That,' he said sternly, 'is for forty-seven years of lousy sex!'

She said nothing, but a few minutes later she prodded him back.

'What was that for?' he asked, shocked.

She said: 'That's for knowing the difference!'

* * *

With a gale-force wind blowing down the street, a police officer noticed an old lady standing on a corner. She was gripping her hat tightly as her skirt blew up around her waist.

He went over to her and said: 'Look, madam, while you're holding on to your precious hat, everybody's getting a good look at everything you have!'

'Listen, sonny,' she replied. 'What they're looking at is eighty-one years old. But this hat is brand new!'

* * *

On her way home from the shops, a woman decided to pay a surprise visit to her grown-up son's house. But when she rang the doorbell, she was shocked to see that it was answered by her daughter-in-law, who was stark naked.

'Oh, it's you,' said the daughter-in-law, hugely embarrassed. 'I was expecting your son. He said he was coming home early from work.'

'But you're completely naked,' said the mother-in-law.

'I know. This is what we call my love dress. Your son adores it. It gets him very excited.'

The mother-in-law was disgusted and quickly left, but the more she thought about how happy the love dress obviously made her son, the more she mellowed. By the time she reached home, she thought it might be just the thing to inject some much-needed romance into her own marriage. So she had a shower, took off all her clothes and lay on the couch waiting for her husband to arrive home.

When her husband walked in, he was alarmed to see her lying there stark naked. 'What's all this?' he barked.

'It's my love dress,' she replied huskily.

'Needs ironing,' he growled. 'What's for dinner?'

* * *

Two male pensioners were talking about sex. One sighed: 'I can't remember the last time I got lucky. It must be years since I last had sex. What about you?'

His friend smiled: 'I'm pleased to say I've still got what it takes to get a woman into the bedroom.'

'Oh, yes? What's that?'

'A stairlift.'

* * *

'Get here as fast as you can,' an old lady shrieked into the telephone. 'A naked stranger is trying to climb in through my apartment window.'

'I'll transfer you to the police department,' said the voice on the other end of the line. 'This is the fire department.'

'I know,' replied the old lady. 'It's the fire department I want. We need a longer ladder!'

* * *

An elderly couple attended their annual medical examination. After giving the husband a thorough health check, the doctor told him: 'You appear to be in good health for your age. Do you have any concerns at all?'

'Well, there is one thing,' he said. 'I find that after I have sex with my wife for the first time I'm usually hot and sweaty. But after I have sex with her for the second time I'm invariably cold and shivery.'

'How unusual,' said the doctor. 'I have no idea what could be causing that. Let me look into it and I'll get back to you if I find anything in my medical books.'

Then the doctor examined the wife. After conducting the standard tests, he told her: 'You seem to be in good health. Any concerns?'

'No, doctor,' she said.

'Oh, okay, it's just that your husband mentioned that after he has sex with you for the first time he feels hot and sweaty, but after he has sex with you for the second time he feels cold and shivery. Do you know why that might be?'

'The silly old fool!' She laughed. 'That's because the first time we have sex is usually in June and the second time is usually in December!'

* * *

Bert and Bill were talking about Viagra. Bill had never heard of it and asked what it was for.

'It's the greatest invention ever,' said Bert. 'It knocks forty years off your life and makes you feel like a man of thirty.'

'Right,' said Bill. 'It sounds wonderful. Can you get it over the counter?'

'Probably, if you took two.'

* * *

A little old lady was staying alone in a motel on her eightieth birthday. Desperate for some company, she decided on impulse to hire a male escort for the evening and soon found a suitable candidate online. His profile picture was mightily impressive and he offered a range of services designed to cater for a woman's every need. Wishing to keep their assignation as anonymous as possible, she chose to call him from the phone in her room.

'Good evening, madam, how may I help you?' said the voice at the other end.

Fearing she would lose her nerve if she hesitated, she got straight to the point. 'Hello,' she said. 'I understand you give delicious sensual massages, so I'd like you to come to my room and caress every inch of my body with oils. Then I want you to ravage me over and over, give me everything you've got and a bit more. I want you to tie me up and have your wicked way with me. Hot and steamy is how I want it, you handsome young stud. How does that sound to you?'

'That sounds absolutely amazing, madam, but you need to press 9 for an outside line.'

* * *

Two old women were discussing their late husbands. One said: 'Did you have mutual orgasms?'

'No,' replied the other. 'I think we were with the Prudential.'

* * *

An old man was asleep in his chair one afternoon when he was woken by the sound of the doorbell. Stirring himself to consciousness, he shuffled falteringly to the front door and opened it to see a beautiful young woman standing there.

'Oh, I'm so sorry,' she said. 'I think I have the wrong house.'

'My dear,' he replied, 'I can assure you that you're at the right house, but you're about forty years too late!'

* * *

While visiting an agricultural show, a retired couple watched the auction of some prize bulls. The auctioneer proudly announced that the first bull had reproduced seventy-two times in the past year.

'Impressive, huh?' said the woman, nudging her husband in the ribs. 'That's six times a month. It's a pity you can't match that.'

The husband said nothing.

The next bull up for auction had reproduced one hundred and forty-four times in the past year.

The woman prodded her husband again. 'Are you listening? That's twelve times a month! You could only dream of that!'

The husband said nothing.

Then a third bull was led in. The auctioneer declared that this bull had reproduced three hundred and sixty-five times in the last year.

The woman elbowed her husband hard in the ribs. 'Three hundred and sixty-five times!' she exclaimed. 'That's every day of the year. That really puts you to shame.'

Finally stung into a response, the husband turned to her and said frostily: 'Yes, but I bet it wasn't all with the same cow.'

4

MONEY DOESN'T GROW ON TREES, YOU KNOW

Feeling uncharacteristically generous, George decided to buy his wife some perfume for her birthday.

Never having bought perfume before, he asked the store assistant if she could recommend a brand suitable for a mature lady. She showed him a bottle that cost a hundred pounds.

'That's a lot more than I was planning to spend,' grumbled George.

So the assistant produced a smaller bottle that cost fifty pounds.

'That's still too expensive,' muttered George.

Despairing at his meanness, but not wanting to lose a sale, the assistant pulled from the display cabinet a tiny bottle that cost only twenty pounds.

'That's still too much,' moaned George. 'Can you show me something cheap?'

And so the assistant handed him a mirror.

* * *

On his deathbed, an old man relayed the details of his will to his wife.

'Marjorie,' he began slowly, 'these are my last wishes.'

'Whatever you want, I'll do,' replied his wife, tenderly holding his hand.

'Thank you,' he continued. 'I want to leave the family business to our son, Alan.'

'Alan?!' protested the wife. 'He has no idea how to run a business. He'll gamble away any profits in the first few months. You know he can't keep out of casinos. Much better to leave the business to your nephew, Jonathan.'

'Very well then, I'll leave it to Jonathan,' agreed the old man. 'So the country cottage I want to leave to our daughter, Linda.'

'Linda?!' shrieked the wife. 'You must be crazy! She's always off travelling abroad. She'd just let the place go to ruin. Better leave that to me.'

'Okay,' said the old man. 'You can have the country cottage. But I want to leave my stamp collection to our grandson, Peter.'

'Why?!' exclaimed the wife. 'Kids these days aren't interested in stamps. Your collection would be wasted on him.'

'Listen, Marjorie,' sighed the old man in exasperation. 'Who's dying here – me or you?'

* * *

A cold caller disturbed an elderly man's afternoon nap. When he finally made it to the door, the woman standing there said: 'Sorry to have disturbed you. I'm collecting for the local swimming pool.'

'Wait there,' said the man brusquely before returning a few moments later with two buckets of water.

* * *

An old farmer and his wife visited an air show. The farmer had always been interested in planes and asked the pilot of a light aircraft how much it would cost for them to be taken up for a ride.

'Three hundred pounds for an hour's ride,' replied the pilot.

'Three hundred?!' exclaimed the farmer. 'There's no way I can afford that, which is a real shame because I've always wanted to go up in one of them things. It would have made my year, let alone my day.'

The pilot was moved by his enthusiasm and took pity on him. 'I'll tell you what I'll do – I'll make a deal with you. You and your wife can ride for free provided you don't make a sound at any point during the flight. But if you do make even the slightest sound, it'll cost you the full three hundred pounds.'

'Okay, it's a deal,' said the farmer, and he and his wife climbed aboard the plane. The pilot went through his entire repertoire, performing a series of spectacular loops, swoops and twists. An hour later as he safely landed the plane, he asked the farmer whether he had enjoyed the experience.

'It was awesome,' gushed the farmer. 'Simply awesome.'

'Well, I want to congratulate you on your bravery,' said the pilot. 'With all those loop-the-loops and sudden dives, I tried my damnedest to get you to make a sound but you managed to remain silent throughout. So you don't have to pay a cent.'

'I appreciate that,' said the farmer, 'but it was a close call. I nearly said something when Maisie fell out forty minutes ago.'

* * *

A husband asked his wife what she wanted for her fortieth wedding anniversary.

'How about a new dress?' he suggested.

'No thanks,' she replied, frostily.

'How about a necklace?'

'No thanks.'

'Maybe a trip to a health spa?'

'No thanks. What I really want is a divorce.'

'Oh,' gasped the husband. 'I wasn't planning on spending that much!'

* * *

An old man who had lived alone all his life asked his accountant to visit him in hospital. He told the accountant: 'When I die, which will probably be soon, I want you to have my remains cremated.'

'And what would you like me to do with your ashes?' asked the accountant.

The old man said: 'I want you to put them in an envelope and mail them to Revenue and Customs with a note saying: "Now you have everything!"'

* * *

Shortly before her sixtieth birthday, a woman said to her husband: 'I had an amazing dream last night where you bought me a beautiful twenty-four-carat gold necklace. What do you think it means?'

With a knowing smile, he replied: 'You'll know on your birthday.'

She could hardly contain her excitement over the next few days, and, sure enough, on the morning of her birthday, her husband reached into his bedside drawer, pulling out a small package. He handed it to her, saying, 'Happy birthday, darling.'

She tore off the paper as fast as she could to reveal a book titled *The Meaning of Dreams*.

* * *

An elderly woman walked into a dentist's practice and asked how much it would cost to extract two teeth.

'Two hundred and fifty pounds,' replied the dentist.

'Two hundred and fifty pounds!' groaned the woman. 'That's a lot of money. Isn't there any way you could do it cheaper?'

'Well,' said the dentist, 'I suppose if you didn't have anaesthetic, I could knock it down to one hundred and eighty.'

'That's still too expensive,' sighed the woman.

The dentist thought for a moment. 'I guess if I save on the anaesthetic and simply rip out the teeth with a pair of pliers, I could cut the price down to a hundred and twenty. But I'm telling you now, it will hurt.'

'That's not a problem,' said the woman. 'Book my husband in for next Thursday.'

* * *

A senior couple were quietly reading one evening when the husband suddenly jumped up and said: 'Put your coat on, Janet. I'm going to the pub.'

'Are you taking me out for a drink?' she said, excitedly.

'Don't be silly,' he replied. 'I'm turning the heating off.'

* * *

Accompanied by her neighbour for emotional support, a woman went to the local police station to report her husband missing. She told the officer: 'He's sixty-two, he's six foot one inch tall with dark wavy hair, athletic build, weighs one hundred and seventy-five pounds and is kind and softly spoken.'

'What are you talking about?' protested the neighbour. 'He's five foot two, grossly overweight, bald as a coot and is a tight-fisted, foul-mouthed drunkard.'

'I know,' said the wife. 'But who wants *him* back?!'

* * *

Having been together for fifty long years, a couple had run out of ideas when it came to buying birthday presents for each other. Aware that his wife no longer drank alcohol or ate chocolates, he was at a loss as to what to buy her, particularly as he didn't want to spend a lot. Then he saw an advert in the local paper offering bargain burial plots at the local cemetery. He thought it would be an unusual yet practical gift and at a price too good to refuse, so he purchased one for her.

However, the following year, he was once more stuck for ideas, so he didn't buy her anything.

'You cheapskate!' she raged. 'Why haven't you bought me a present for my birthday?'

'I don't know what you're complaining about,' he replied. 'You still haven't used the present I got you last year.'

* * *

A grandfather was notoriously mean with his money, but, when challenged about the quality of gifts that he bought for his grandson, he would always offer the excuse of not wanting to spoil the boy.

Matters came to a head on the boy's tenth birthday. Instead of the usual tiny bag of sweets from Grandpa, there was a large, neatly wrapped box. What might it contain? Something exciting surely?

For once it looked as though Grandpa had come up trumps.

With mounting anticipation, the boy hurriedly unwrapped the paper to reveal a large shoebox. But when he removed the lid of the box, there was nothing inside. The box was empty.

'What's this, Grandpa,' asked the boy, fighting back tears.

The old man said: 'It's an Action Man deserter.'

* * *

Frank complained to his friend: 'My wife is always asking me for more money. Last month she asked me for a hundred pounds; last week she wanted two hundred; and yesterday it was four hundred pounds.'

'What does she do with it all?' asked the friend.

'I don't know,' said Frank. 'I never give her any.'

* * *

An elderly couple were shopping in the supermarket. When he reached the drinks section the husband picked up two packs of beer and put them in his shopping cart.

'What do you think you're doing?' asked his wife.

'They're on special offer,' he pleaded. 'Only twelve pounds fifty for twelve cans.'

'I don't care,' said his wife. 'We can't afford them. Put them back.'

He did as he was told.

A few aisles further on, she picked up a twenty-five-pound jar of face cream and put it in the cart.

'What do you think you're doing?' asked the husband indignantly.

'It's my face cream,' she said. 'It makes me look beautiful.'

'So do twelve cans of beer,' he said. 'And they're half the price!'

* * *

An old man was always careful with his money, but one year he was forced to loosen the purse strings when his wife demanded a diamond ring for their sixtieth wedding anniversary. However, when she opened the gift box, she was distinctly unimpressed.

'Why did you buy me such a tiny diamond?' she complained.

He said: 'I didn't want the glare to hurt your eyes.'

* * *

A young man was studying an elderly couple in McDonald's. He saw that they had ordered one cheeseburger, a side order of fries and a soft drink with an extra cup. He watched the old man carefully cut the cheeseburger in half before dividing the fries into two equal portions. Then the old man poured half of the soft drink into the extra cup and started to eat.

Concluding that the reason they had to divide everything up was because they could not afford to pay for two meals, the young man took pity on them. He went over to their table and offered them five pounds so that they could buy a second meal.

'No, you don't understand,' said the old man. 'It's not that we can't afford it – this is just the way we've always done things and always will. We've been married for over fifty years, and we always share everything.'

'I see,' said the young man who then turned to the old woman and asked if she was going to eat.

'Not yet, sonny,' she answered. 'It's his turn with the teeth.'

* * *

A man decided to buy his partner a beautiful diamond ring for her sixtieth birthday. Hearing about this, a friend of his said: 'But I thought she always wanted a fancy four-wheel-drive vehicle?'

'She did,' he replied. 'But where was I going to find a fake Land Rover?'

* * *

An old man was lying on his deathbed, surrounded by his family. Summoning his last ounce of strength, he lifted his head and whispered: 'Is my beloved wife, Joan, here?'

'Yes, I am here,' said his wife.

'And are my dear children, Simon and Monica, here, too?'

'Yes, father,' they replied. 'We are here.'

'And are my darling grandchildren, Sam, Kirsty and Holly, with me as well?'

'Yes, Grandad,' they said. 'We are all here with you at your bedside.'

The old man laid his head back down on the pillow and said: 'So... if everybody is here, why is the light on in the kitchen?'

5

A FEW ONE-LINERS... THAT YOU MAY EVEN BE ABLE TO REMEMBER

Why was the senior driver speeding? To get where he was going before he forgot where he was going.

* * *

Did you hear about the woman who called her elderly husband Spiderman? He hasn't got any super powers, he just has trouble getting out of the bath.

* * *

The best way to get your husband to do something is to suggest he's too old to do it.

* * *

Two old men were having an argument. One said: 'I'm so angry, I'm taking you off my pallbearer list!'

* * *

Why don't seniors need to go to the gym? They get plenty of exercise from walking down memory lane.

* * *

Having sex in your late seventies is still great. It just gets more difficult to see who you're having it with.

* * *

My wife always used to say, 'Sixty is the new thirty.' Lovely woman... banned from driving.

* * *

When you're twenty and you drop something, you pick it up. When you're eighty and you drop something, you decide you don't need it any more.

6

BELIEVE IT OR NOT, I WAS YOUNG ONCE

An elderly gentleman and a young man were pushing their trolleys around the supermarket aisles when they accidentally collided. Both apologised profusely.

'I was looking for my wife,' explained the old man, 'and I guess I wasn't looking where I was going.'

'Same here,' said the younger man. 'My wife was here a minute ago, but she's disappeared off somewhere. I'm trying to find her. She can't be far away.'

'Perhaps we can help each other,' suggested the old man. 'What does your wife look like?'

'She's twenty-five, she has blonde hair, she's quite tall with long, slim legs and blue eyes. She's wearing a short, black skirt, a tight-fitting red top and knee-length black boots. What does your wife look like?'

'Oh, never mind,' replied the old man. 'Let's look for yours first.'

* * *

A newly retired man bought a home near the local school. He spent the first few weeks of his retirement in blissful peace but then the new school year began. From then on, the same group of boys made a fearful racket on their way home from school each day, banging loudly on every bin in the street.

Eventually the old man could bear it no longer, so he devised a plan. He decided to confront the boys one afternoon as they banged their way down his street. 'You kids are a lot of fun,' he said. 'I used to do the same thing when I was your age. Will you do me a favour? I'll give you each a pound if you promise to come round here every day and bang on the bins.'

The boys were more than happy with the arrangement and continued to bang on the bins every day on their walk home.

Then a week later, the old man greeted the boys again, but this time he wasn't smiling. 'The rising cost of living is really starting to hit me,' he said. 'I only have my pension to rely on. I'm sorry, but I can't afford to pay you so much. I'm going to have to cut it down to fifty pence a day for you to keep banging on the bins.'

The boys weren't overjoyed, but accepted the deal as they were still getting paid for having fun.

Then, a few days later, the old man approached them again. 'Listen,' he said. 'Money is tighter than ever. I'm afraid in future I can only afford to give you twenty-five pence each to keep banging on the bins.'

'What?!' said the boys' leader. 'You must be joking! There's no way we're going to waste our time banging on these bins for twenty-five measly pence. That's it, mister. We quit!'

And the old man enjoyed peace and serenity for the rest of his days.

* * *

A man in his forties found himself still living at home with his overbearing mother. Whenever he had come close to meeting a girl he might consider settling down with, his mother had always managed to scupper the relationship. Her excuse was that no girl was good enough for her precious son. As the years ticked by, he eventually realised that unless he acted soon he would end up living at home forever, so one evening he plucked up the courage to announce: 'Mother, I have fallen in love and intend getting married. I'm going to bring three ladies to the house tomorrow evening and you have to guess which one I'm going to marry.'

'If I have to,' muttered his mother, scarcely hiding her annoyance.

The following evening, the son brought three attractive women into the living room and asked them to sit down. 'Right, Mother,' he said, 'which of these young ladies do you think is the one that I'm going to marry?'

Without hesitation, the mother pointed her finger and replied: 'The one in the middle.'

'That's right!' said the son. 'How did you know?'

'Because I don't like her.'

* * *

A son treated his elderly father to lunch in a restaurant. When the young waitress came to the table to take their order, the old man turned to her and said: 'Can I have a quickie, miss? I really fancy a quickie.'

The son rolled his eyes, leaned across and whispered: 'Dad, it's pronounced "quiche".'

* * *

A small boy and his grandfather were raking leaves in the garden when the boy noticed an earthworm trying to wriggle back into its hole.

'Grandad,' he said, 'I bet I can put that worm back in that hole.'

'I'll bet you five pounds you can't,' said the grandfather. 'The worm's too soft and limp to go into that hole. You'll never get it in.'

But the boy had an idea. He went into the house, returned with a can of hairspray and sprayed the worm until it became straight and stiff. Then he stuffed the worm back into the hole.

Suitably impressed, his grandfather gave him the five pounds and went indoors with a broad grin on his face. Thirty minutes later, he reappeared and handed his grandson another five pounds.

'But, Grandad, you already gave me five pounds.'

'I know. That's from your Grandma.'

* * *

A retired man was working out in the gym when he spotted a beautiful young woman who was less than half his age.

He asked his trainer: 'What machine do you think I should use to impress a girl like that?'

The trainer replied: 'I'd try the ATM in the lobby.'

* * *

A man in Boston received a surprise call from his elderly father in Miami. 'David,' began the father ominously, 'I've decided that I'm going to divorce your mother.'

'What do you mean?' said David, reeling from the revelation. 'You can't get a divorce. You two have been married for forty-two years.'

'I'm sorry,' said the father, 'but that's the way it is. My mind is made up. I don't want to discuss it and you won't talk me out of it but I just thought I should let you know.'

'Well, can I at least talk to Mum?' asked David.

'No,' replied his father bluntly. 'I don't want you talking to her, because I haven't told her yet. But I'm seeing a lawyer the day after tomorrow.'

David could not believe what he was hearing. His parents had always appeared to be happy together. There must be something he could do. 'Listen, Dad,' he pleaded. 'Don't do anything hasty. You can't destroy the family and everything you've worked so hard for just on impulse. I'll catch the first available flight down and we can all talk it over calmly and responsibly before you start going to see lawyers. Does that sound reasonable?'

'I guess so,' said the father, hesitantly. 'I'll postpone the appointment with the lawyer for a couple of days until we know where we're at. Will you call your sister and break the news to her? I really don't want to have to go over it all again to someone else.'

Within an hour the father had received a phone call from his daughter in Chicago. She said that she and her brother had already purchased plane tickets online and that they and their children would be arriving in Miami the following evening. She, too, made him promise not to do anything rash in the meantime.

The father promised and put down the phone. He then turned to his wife and said: 'Well, darling, it worked. But what are we going to have to do to get them to come down next year?'

* * *

A grandmother was giving directions to her grown-up grandson who was coming to visit her. 'Right, Joseph, you come to the front door of the block of flats. There is an intercom on the right-hand side of the door. Use your elbow to push button nine. I will buzz you in. Come inside, and you will see the lift on the left. Step in, and with your elbow press the button for the third floor. When you get out at the third floor, my flat is the second on the left. With your elbow, press my doorbell.'

'Okay, Grandma,' he replied. 'That sounds straight-forward enough. But tell me, why do I need to press all those buttons with my elbow?'

The grandmother replied: 'You're not coming empty-handed, are you?'

* * *

An old-timer was sitting on his porch in Tennessee when a young man approached him holding a pen and clipboard.

'What are you selling, son?' the old man grumbled.

'I'm not selling anything,' said the young man. 'I'm the census-taker.'

'The what?'

'The census-taker. We're trying to find out how many people there are in the United States.'

'No use asking me,' said the old man, 'because I'm damned if I know!'

* * *

An elderly man was staying at an expensive city hotel. At his second breakfast there, he summoned the young waiter and said: 'I want some scrambled eggs with bits of shell in them, toast that is burnt to a cinder and a cup of coffee that tastes like mud.'

'I'm sorry, sir,' said the young waiter, 'we don't serve breakfast like that.'

'Well,' snapped the old man, 'you did yesterday!'

* * *

A man in his late thirties was still living with his parents. It was a fractious relationship and there were frequent rows, particularly between the son and his mother. After one bitter confrontation, the son yelled at his parents: 'That's it! I've had enough. I want excitement, adventure, money and beautiful women. I'll never find that here at home, so I'm leaving. Don't try to stop me!'

With that, he grabbed his car keys and headed for the door. His father followed him into the hallway.

'Didn't you hear what I said?' said the son. 'I don't want you to try to stop me.'

'Who's trying to stop you?' replied the father. 'If you hang on a minute, I'll join you.'

* * *

A boy was struggling with his maths homework. 'Grandpa,' he begged, 'could you help me with this?'

'I could,' replied his grandfather, adopting the moral high ground, 'but it wouldn't be right, would it?'

'I don't suppose it would, Grandpa,' sighed the boy, 'but have a shot at it anyway.'

* * *

Audrey and Edna were talking about their respective grandchildren. Audrey said sadly: 'Every year I send gifts, greeting cards and cheques to my grandchildren, but they hardly ever bother to visit me.'

'I send cheques to my grandchildren, too,' said Edna, 'and they visit me regularly.'

'You're so lucky to have considerate grand-children,' sighed Audrey.

Edna smiled. 'My grandchildren are really no different from yours.'

'So what do you do that's different?' asked Audrey. 'Are the cheques you write bigger than mine?'

'No,' chuckled Edna. 'I just don't sign mine.'

* * *

Three men in their seventies were discussing what they would like their grandchildren to be saying about them in fifty years' time.

The first man said: 'I'd like my grandchildren to say, "He was a great businessman."'

The second man said: 'I'd like my grandchildren to say, "He was a wonderful husband and father."'

Then they turned to the third man and asked:

'What would you like your grandchildren to be saying about you in fifty years' time?'

The third man leaned back in his chair and replied: 'I'd like them to say, "He still looks good for his age!"'

* * *

While writing at a post office desk, a young man was approached by an elderly gentleman holding a postcard. 'Excuse me, young man,' he said. 'Would you mind addressing this postcard for me? My arthritis is really bad today and I can hardly hold a pen.'

'No problem,' said the young man, and he wrote down the address given to him.

'Also,' added the old man, 'would you be kind enough to write a short message on the card and to sign it for me?'

'Yes, okay,' said the young man, and he patiently wrote the message that the old man dictated to him. When he had finished, he handed the card to the old man and said: 'There, that's it. Done. Is there anything else I can help you with?'

'Yes,' said the old man, glancing at the card. 'At the end, could you add: "PS, please excuse the sloppy handwriting."'

* * *

A little boy said to his grandfather: 'Make a frog noise for me, Grandad.'

'No,' said the old man grumpily, 'I don't feel like making a frog noise right now.'

'Oh, please, Grandad, make a frog noise.'

'No, I don't want to.'

'Pleeeease, Grandad! Make a frog noise.'

'Why is it such a big deal for me to make a frog noise?'

'Because Dad says when you croak we can go to Disneyworld.'

* * *

An extremely wealthy seventy-year-old widower walked slowly into a bar with a glamorous twenty-something girl on his arm. She appeared to be besotted with him and hung on his every word.

His friends at the bar were naturally envious and, when she left to powder her nose, they asked him how he had managed to acquire such a stunning girlfriend.

'Oh, she's not my girlfriend,' he explained. 'She's my wife.'

'What?!' exclaimed the friends in unison. 'How the hell did you manage to persuade her to marry you?'

'I lied about my age,' he said.

'You mean you told her you were only fifty?'

'No.' He smiled. 'I told her I was ninety.'

7

EVERYONE IN THIS PLACE IS SO OLD

A woman visited her elderly father in a retirement home. She was pleased to see him looking perkier than usual and he said that was because he had been sleeping much better of late.

'I think it's the new medication they've been giving me,' he enthused. 'It really seems to have helped.'

'What is this new medication?' she inquired.

'Every night they give me a glass of warm milk and a Viagra tablet.'

'Viagra!' said the daughter, shocked. 'Why are they giving you that?'

'I have no idea,' he said.

As she was leaving, the daughter asked the nurse on duty about the new medication.

'The warm milk helps him sleep,' explained the nurse.

'Yes, I can understand that,' said the daughter. 'But what about the Viagra?'

'Oh,' said the nurse. 'That's to stop him rolling out of bed.'

* * *

An elderly lady was settling into her new life in a retirement home. On her first morning there, the nurses gently bathed her and gave her a healthy breakfast before placing her in a comfortable armchair next to a window that overlooked a pretty garden. She smiled and appeared content but after a few minutes she began to lean sideways in her chair.

Seeing this, two staff members rushed across and straightened her up.

She seemed fine, but, a few minutes later, her body started to lean to the other side. Once again, the nurses hurried over to catch her and straighten her up. This was repeated several times through the course of the morning.

In the afternoon, her family arrived to see how she was dealing with her new surroundings. 'Are they treating you well in here?' she asked.

'Yes, it's quite nice,' she replied. 'Except they won't let you fart!'

* * *

Eleanor and Kathleen were two elderly widows living in a retirement home. Over the course of a few weeks, they became intrigued by a new arrival at the home: a quiet, distinguished gentleman who carried a certain air of mystery about him.

One day, Eleanor said to her friend: 'Kathleen, you know how shy I am. Why don't you go over and chat to him to see if you can find out more about him? He looks very lonely.'

So Kathleen crossed the lounge to talk to the man, who was sitting by the window quietly reading a book. 'I'm sorry to interrupt your reading,' she began, 'but my friend and I were wondering why you always look so lonely.'

'It's no surprise that I'm alone in the world,' he replied, sadly, putting down his book. 'You see, I've spent the last thirty years of my life in prison.'

'Oh!' said Kathleen. 'What happened?'

'I strangled my third wife.'

'Oh! What happened to your second wife?'

'I shot her.'

'And what about your first wife?'

'We had a fight and she fell from the fifteenth floor of our block of flats.'

'Oh, my!'

Then Kathleen turned to her friend across the room and called out: 'Yoo hoo, Eleanor! It's okay. He's single!'

* * *

Ted Danson paid a charity visit to a retirement home in order to cheer up the elderly residents. But he was dismayed that none of them seemed to recognise him. Instead, they all looked bewildered. Finally, he went over to one old lady and said: 'Do you know who I am?'

'Don't worry, dear,' whispered the old lady. 'Matron will tell you.'

* * *

An old man and an old woman were sitting in the living room of their retirement home. Suddenly the old man said to the old woman: 'I bet you can't guess how old I am.'

The old lady said: 'I'll give it a shot. Let me try something.'

With that, she put her hand down his pants and began feeling his privates for a few seconds before announcing: 'You're eighty-six.'

'That's unbelievable!' he exclaimed. 'How did you know?'

She said: 'You told me yesterday!'

* * *

A pastor visited an elderly parishioner who was confined to bed at her retirement home. While a nurse was tending to the old lady, the pastor spotted a bowl of peanuts on the bedside table and helped himself to a handful. When the nurse had finished, he continued dipping into the peanuts. Eventually he realised that the bowl was empty.

'I'm so sorry, Mrs Clements,' he said. 'I appear to have eaten all of your delicious peanuts.'

'Don't worry,' replied the old lady. 'They would just have sat there anyway. Without my teeth, all I can do is suck the chocolate off and put them back in the bowl!'

* * *

A ninety-year-old woman tottered into the recreation room of a retirement home and, holding her clenched fist aloft, declared: 'Anyone who can guess what's in my hand can sleep with me tonight.'

An uninterested old man called out: 'An elephant.'

'That's near enough,' grinned the woman.

* * *

Two elderly men were relaxing in the living room of their retirement home. As they started reminiscing about past relationships, one of the men pulled out his phone and showed the other a photo.

'That was my first wife,' he said.

'She's very attractive,' said the other.

'If you think she's attractive, you should see my second wife!'

'Why? Is she beautiful too?'

'No, she's an optician.'

* * *

A woman visited her elderly father in a retirement home. No sooner had she sat down than another resident entered the ward, waving his arms around and making beeping noises.

'Excuse me,' said the woman. 'What are you doing?'

'I'm driving my car,' he replied cheerily. 'Beep, beep! Beep, beep!'

'But you're walking around the living room of a retirement home,' explained the woman. 'You're not driving a car.'

'Don't tell him that,' hissed the woman's father. 'He pays me ten pounds a week to clean it!'

* * *

Millicent, a widow in her fifties, signed up to an online dating site. After her first date, she reported back to her sister.

'How did it go?' asked the sister.

'It was awful,' said Millicent. 'He showed up in a 1942 Rolls-Royce.'

'What's wrong with that?'

Millicent replied: 'He was the original owner.'

* * *

Mavis and Gertrude had stepped out of their retirement home for a cigarette when it started to rain. Mavis immediately delved into her handbag, pulled out a condom, cut off the end, put it over her cigarette and continued smoking.

'What's that?' asked Gertrude

'It's a condom,' said Mavis. 'I put one over my cigarette when it's raining and it keeps the cigarette dry.'

'How ingenious! Where did you get it?'

'They sell them at the chemist down the road.'

So, the next day, Gertrude caught a bus to the chemist and asked the pharmacist for a pack of condoms.

'Any particular brand?' asked the pharmacist.

'It doesn't matter,' said Gertrude. 'Just as long as it fits a Camel.'

The pharmacist fainted.

* * *

Two old men were sitting in the garden of their retirement home. One turned to the other and said: 'I'm eighty-four years old now and I've got so many aches and pains all over my body. It's tough just living from day to day. You're the same age as me. How do you feel?'

'Actually,' replied his friend. 'I feel just like a newborn baby.'

'Really?'

'Yes. No hair, no teeth, and I think I've just wet my pants.'

* * *

Three old ladies were sitting in their retirement home, reminiscing about the good old days. The first old lady recalled how, in the days before supermarkets, she used to shop for fresh vegetables at the local grocer's store. Using her hands, she proceeded to demonstrate the length and thickness of a cucumber that she could buy for a few pennies.

The second old lady nodded in agreement, adding that onions also used to be much bigger and cheaper than today. She then cupped her hands to demonstrate the size and weight of two large onions that she used to be able to buy for a few pennies.

Watching all this, the third old lady said: 'I can't hear a word you're saying, but I remember the guy you're talking about.'

8

YOU KNOW YOU'RE GETTING OLD WHEN...

You can't walk past a bathroom without thinking, 'I may as well have a pee while I'm here.'

* * *

You refer to your knees as 'good' and 'bad' rather than 'left' and 'right'.

* * *

At breakfast you hear snap, crackle and pop even when you're not eating cereal.

* * *

It takes at least two attempts to get up from the sofa.

* * *

Your knees buckle, but your belt won't.

* * *

You wake up looking like your driver's licence picture.

* * *

Your mind makes contracts that your body can't meet.

* * *

You wake up with that 'morning after' feeling when there was no 'night before'.

* * *

You turn out the lights for economic rather than romantic reasons.

* * *

Your idea of 'happy hour' is a nap.

* * *

You have a party and the neighbours don't even notice.

* * *

You have to scroll for ever in drop-down menus to find your year of birth.

* * *

You and your teeth no longer sleep together.

9

WE'VE BEEN TOGETHER 40 YEARS – 62 WITH THE WIND-CHILL FACTOR

As she lay dying in bed, an old woman's thoughts turned to her impending funeral. She summoned her husband and asked him: 'What flowers were you planning on getting for my service?'

'Lilies,' he said.

'Never,' she snapped. 'I hate lilies. I want roses – white roses. Make sure you remember.'

'Yes, dear, I will,' he replied meekly.

'And how many cars do you intend ordering?'

'I thought maybe three.'

'Too many. A waste of money. Cancel one.'

'Very well, dear.'

'And I want you to travel in the same car as my sister.'

'But,' he protested, 'you know that she and I don't get on. We haven't spoken in years.'

'Just do it,' ordered the wife.

'If that's what you want,' he sighed, 'I'll do it. But I'm telling you, it will spoil the day for me.'

* * *

A couple who had been together for four decades were entertaining friends one evening when the subject of the conversation turned to relationship counselling.

'That's not something we would ever need,' said the wife confidently. 'Robert and I have a wonderful relationship. It's all a matter of education.'

'How do you mean?' asked one of the friends.

'Well, you see, at college, Robert studied communications and I did drama. So he is really good at communicating and I can act like I'm listening.'

* * *

Two old women met in the street. After the usual discussion about their health and what operations they had undergone in the past twelve months, the conversation turned to their respective husbands.

'Oh,' said one. 'Didn't you know? My Sid died last month. He went out to the garden to dig up some fresh carrots for dinner, had a heart attack and dropped dead on the spot.'

'Oh no!' exclaimed the other. 'What did you do?'

'What could I do?! I opened a tin of peas instead.'

* * *

After nearly forty years of marriage, a wife was feeling a little neglected and needed reassurance that her husband still loved her. 'If I were to die tomorrow,' she said to him, 'and you remarried, would you give your new wife my jewellery?'

'What an awful thing to ask!' exclaimed the husband. 'No, of course I wouldn't.'

'And would you give her any of my clothes?'

'I can't believe you're asking me that, darling,' he said, aggrieved. 'But no, of course I wouldn't.'

'What about my golf clubs?'

'Absolutely not,' said the husband emphatically. 'She's left-handed.'

* * *

An elderly man walked into a shoe shop and asked for a pair of size eight shoes.

The sales assistant took one look at the customer's feet and said: 'Are you sure, sir? You look more like a size eleven to me.'

The old man barked: 'Just bring me size eight.'

So the assistant fetched a pair of size eight shoes and the old man just about managed to squeeze his feet into them. But as soon as he tried to walk, it was clear that he was in considerable pain.

The assistant was puzzled. 'Sir, why are you so insistent about wearing undersized shoes?'

'If you must know,' said the old man, 'my business went bust, I lost my house, I live with my mother-in-law, my wife is having an affair with my best friend, my son has joined a weird religious sect and my daughter is pregnant by a convicted bank robber. So the only pleasure I still have in life is taking these damn shoes off!'

* * *

A retired gentleman went to apply for Social Security. The woman behind the counter asked him for his driver's licence so that she could verify his age, but, as he searched through his pockets, he realised that he had forgotten to bring any form of ID. He apologised and said he would go home and come back later.

'That won't be necessary,' she said. 'If you unbutton your shirt, I can get an idea of your age.'

So, he unbuttoned his shirt to reveal multiple tufts of grey chest hair.

'That silver hair is proof enough for me,' she said, and she processed his application.

When he got home, he told his wife about his experience at the Social Security office. She looked at him and said: 'You should have dropped your pants – you might have qualified for disability, too.'

* * *

Lionel and Brenda were sitting on the sofa watching TV one evening when Lionel suddenly put his arm around Brenda. Since they had been together for more than thirty-five years, this was an unexpectedly romantic gesture. Then, slowly, his hand began to caress her hip, before moving down to her outer thigh, gently tracing every inch of skin. Still without saying a word, he moved his hand to explore her inner thigh, causing Brenda to feel quite giddy. Next, his hand crossed to the other thigh, massaging every crease and crevice, the touch of his fingers making her whole body tingle. As his hand circled her groin, she was becoming increasingly aroused and let out an audible gasp, but just as she turned to face him in readiness for a passionate kiss, he pulled his hand away.

'Lionel, why have you stopped?' she asked, breath-lessly.

He said: 'I've found the remote.'

* * *

A grumpy old man took his dog to the veterinarian and asked the vet to cut off its tail.

'Why do you want to do that?' asked the vet.

'Because my wife's sister is arriving tomorrow, and I don't want anything to make her think she's welcome.'

* * *

Driving home after a night out, a retired couple were stopped by a police officer.

Addressing the husband, who was driving, the officer began: 'Did you know you were speeding, sir?'

'No, I didn't know, officer,' said the husband.

'Of course you did,' interrupted the wife. 'You're always speeding. You have no regard for anyone's safety, least of all mine.'

The officer then inspected the rear of the car. 'And did you know one of your brake lights is broken, sir?'

'No, officer,' said the husband. 'I didn't know that it was broken.'

'Of course you knew it was broken,' said the wife, interrupting once more. 'I've been on at you for weeks to get it fixed, but you never have. Everything's always too much trouble for you.'

Amazed at the wife's behaviour, the officer began to sympathise with the husband and asked him: 'Does she always talk to you like this?'

To which the wife replied: 'Only when he's drunk.'

* * *

A husband was accompanying his wife to her old school reunion. He couldn't take his eyes off a dishevelled drunk who was sitting alone at a table in the corner. Eventually he asked his wife: 'Do you know him?'

'I do,' she replied. 'He's my old boyfriend. I believe he started drinking right after we broke up over forty years ago, and apparently he's never been sober since.'

'Wow!' exclaimed her husband. 'You wouldn't think someone could go on celebrating that long!'

* * *

On a warm summer afternoon, a lazy old-timer and his equally idle wife were sitting in their rocking chairs on the porch at the side of their house when they heard a funeral procession pass by the front door.

'That'll be old Alec's funeral,' said the husband. 'They reckon it's the biggest there's been round these parts for years.'

'I'd like to have seen it,' said the wife.

'Me too. After all, he was best man at our wedding.'

'That's right. Shame we ain't facin' that way!'

* * *

A husband and wife were lying in bed when the husband turned to his wife and said gloomily: 'Do you remember fifty years ago when your father caught us behind the barn and we were stark naked?'

'I do remember,' said the wife.

'And do you remember what your father told me that day?'

'No, I don't recall.'

'Well, I do. He said that if I didn't marry you, he would have me locked up in prison for fifty years.'

'Really? So why are you looking so sad?'

'I've just realised I would have been a free man by now.'

* * *

After nearly forty years together, a couple's relationship was starting to show signs of strain. So they went to see a marriage counsellor, a man who came highly recommended. He listened patiently while the wife outlined her grievances, the main one being that her husband neglected her.

'He no longer seems to take any interest in me,' she said. 'And he certainly never shows me any affection.'

Hearing this, the husband merely shrugged his shoulders, so the counsellor decided to take drastic action and went over to the wife and kissed her passionately on the lips. As the wife slumped back in her seat in shock, the counsellor turned to the husband and said: 'Your wife needs that at least twice a week.'

'Well,' said the husband, 'I can get her here Mondays and Wednesdays.'

* * *

Two old ladies were chatting over coffee. One asked: 'What are you going to get your husband for your twenty-fifth wedding anniversary?'

'I was thinking about buying him a trip to Australia,' said the other. 'He's always wanted to go.'

'A trip to Australia! That's really something. But how will you be able to top that for your thirtieth anniversary?'

'I'm not sure. Maybe I'll pay for his plane ticket back.'

* * *

A couple in their sixties were driving home from a party. Suddenly the wife turned to her husband and said: 'Have I ever told you how sexy and irresistible to women you are?'

'I don't believe you have, dear,' replied the husband, surprised and flattered.

She glared back at him. 'Then what on earth gave you that idea at the party?'

* * *

While driving her husband to the airport, an elderly woman was pulled over by a traffic cop. The officer climbed out of his car and began to quiz her. Addressing her through the driver's window, he asked: 'Did you know you were speeding, ma'am?'

The old woman turned to her husband and barked: 'What did he say?'

The husband shouted: 'He says you were speeding.'

'May I see your licence, ma'am?' said the officer.

'What did he say?' said the old woman.

'He wants to see your licence,' shouted the husband.

She handed the officer her driver's licence, which he proceeded to study carefully.

'I see you're from Boise, Idaho,' said the officer. 'I spent some time there once. I remember I had the worst sex there with any woman I've had in my entire life.'

'What did he say?' said the old woman.

The husband yelled: 'He thinks he knows you.'

* * *

For her sixty-fifth birthday, a woman was given a range of expensive creams and cosmetics designed to make her look years younger. After applying them all, she asked her grumpy husband: 'Darling, tell me honestly. What age do you think I look?'

Peering over his newspaper, he said: 'From your skin, twenty-five; your hair, twenty-three; and your figure, twenty-five.'

'Oh, that's the nicest thing you've ever said to me,' she said, smiling.

'Wait a second,' he said. 'I haven't added them up yet!'

* * *

Jean bumped into her friend Cynthia while out shopping. She immediately noticed that Cynthia was wearing a new locket around her neck.

'Does it have some sort of memento inside?' asked Jean.

'Yes, it's a lock of my husband's hair,' replied Cynthia.

'But Peter is still alive, isn't he?'

'I know, but his hair is gone.'

* * *

An old woman went to see a lawyer about getting a divorce.

The lawyer asked: 'What grounds do you have, madam?'

'About seven acres,' she replied.

'Sorry,' said the lawyer, 'I think you misunderstood my question. Let me rephrase it: do you have a grudge?'

'No,' said the old woman, 'just a parking space.'

'I'll try again,' said the lawyer, through gritted teeth. 'Does your husband beat you up?'

'No,' said the old woman, 'I always get up at least an hour before he does.'

The lawyer could see that he was getting nowhere. 'Madam,' he said, 'are you sure you want a divorce?'

'I'm not the one who wants a divorce,' she replied. 'My husband does. For some reason he claims we never communicate.'

* * *

An elderly couple were celebrating their golden wedding anniversary when the husband suddenly turned to his wife and said: 'My dear, there is something that has been troubling me for many years: Why does our seventh child not look remotely like the rest of our children? I have always wanted to ask you about it and I don't think I can put aside my concerns and suspicions any longer. You have been a kind, dutiful wife for all these years but please tell me, does Giles have a different father?'

The wife held her head in shame, unable to look her husband in the eye. Finally she admitted:

'Yes, Giles does have a different father from our six other children.'

The husband was distraught. After letting the devastating news sink in for a minute or two, he asked her tearfully: 'So who was it? Who is Giles's real father?'

The wife looked back at him and replied, shakily: 'You, darling.'

* * *

Although she wasn't always the best cook, an elderly woman loved to try out new recipes on her long-suffering husband, often with disastrous results. One evening, she decided to bake him a homemade lasagne. After he had taken the first hesitant mouthful, she waited eagerly for his reaction. When he said nothing, she asked hopefully: 'If I baked this lasagne commercially, how much do you think I would get it for it?'

Still trying to chew through the pasta, he replied: 'About ten years.'

* * *

One day a grumpy old git asked his wife: 'How come you never get mad when we argue? How do you always manage to control your temper?'

'I clean the toilet,' she replied.

'How does that help?' he asked.

She said: 'I use your toothbrush.'

* * *

An elderly woman decided to hire an artist to paint her portrait. At the first session, she issued clear instructions. 'I want you to paint me wearing large diamond earrings, a splendid diamond necklace, a gold bracelet, an emerald brooch and an expensive gold watch.'

'But you're not wearing any of those things,' said the artist, puzzled.

'I know,' said the woman. 'It's just in case I die before my husband. If that were to happen, I'm sure he would quickly remarry and I want to drive his new wife crazy looking for all that jewellery!'

* * *

Two men in their late sixties were playing a round of golf at their local course. One of them was about to play his approach shot to the green when he saw a funeral procession on the road that ran alongside the course. He immediately stopped in mid-swing, took off his cap, closed his eyes and bowed his head in prayer.

After the funeral procession had passed, his playing partner went over to him and said: 'That was a really nice gesture from you. I hadn't realised what a compassionate, considerate man you are.'

'It was nothing really. And besides, I was married to her for forty-one years.'

* * *

At breakfast one morning, an old lady gazed longingly at her husband and said: 'Just think, darling, we've been married for fifty years now.'

'That's true,' he replied. 'Fifty years ago, we were sitting together at this same breakfast table. And we were probably stark naked.'

'Well,' said the old woman excitedly, 'what do you say we get naked again for old time's sake?'

So they both stripped off and sat back down at the table. 'Do you know,' the old woman said breathlessly, 'my breasts are as hot for you today as they were fifty years ago? I can feel them tingling.'

'I'm not surprised,' said the husband. 'One's in your coffee and the other's in your porridge!'

* * *

As he lay on his deathbed, a husband summoned up the strength to gasp to his wife: 'Please grant me one last wish.'

'Of course, my dearest,' she said. 'What is it?

'Six months after I die, I want you to marry Dennis from next door.'

'But I thought you hated Dennis,' she said.

'I do.' He smiled.

* * *

Martin and Mary, a widower and a widow in their late eighties, had decided to get married. While out for a stroll one afternoon to discuss their wedding plans, they entered a chemist.

Martin went up to the counter and asked the pharmacist: 'Do you stock blood-pressure tablets?'

'Yes,' replied the pharmacist.

'And what about pills to lower cholesterol?'

'Of course, no problem,' said the pharmacist.

Then Mary chimed in: 'And do you sell arthritis remedies?'

'Yes, we do,' said the pharmacist.

'And medication for cataracts?'

'Yes, we've got that, too.'

'Sleeping pills, indigestion tablets, ear drops...?'

'All in stock.'

'Wheelchairs and walkers?'

'All makes and sizes.'

'Right,' said Martin to the pharmacist. 'We'd like to register here for our wedding gifts.'

* * *

A senior couple were lying in bed one night. The husband was on the verge of falling asleep but the wife was in a nostalgic, romantic mood and wanted to talk.

She said: 'Remember how you used to hold my hand when we were courting?'

Wearily, he reached across, held her hand for a second and then tried to get back to sleep.

A few moments later, she whispered: 'Then you used to kiss me.'

Mildly irritated, he leaned over, gave her a quick peck on the cheek and settled down to sleep.

Thirty seconds later, she said: 'Then you used to bite my neck.'

Angrily he threw back the duvet and clambered out of bed.

'Where are you going?' she asked.

'To get my teeth!'

* * *

Lying in his bedroom on his deathbed, an elderly man smelled the aroma of his favourite chocolate-chip cookies wafting up the stairs. Mustering his last reserves of energy, he slowly hauled himself out of bed and staggered out of the bedroom. Gripping the handrail as best he could, he breathlessly made his way down the stairs and stumbled into the kitchen. There, his eyes lit up as he saw half a dozen trays of freshly baked cookies spread out on the table. Thinking that they must be a parting gift from his beloved, he reached out to take one. But as he did so, he received a sharp rap across the hand from a spatula.

'Leave those alone!' snapped his wife. 'They're for the funeral.'

Introduction

Some 4,500 years ago, a sandstorm overwhelmed a village at the Bay of Skaill in Orkney. People were forced to flee from their houses abandoning most of their possessions. In a hurry to leave through the low door of her home, one woman broke her necklace and left behind on the floor a stream of beads.

In 1850, another storm ripped open the sand dunes to expose some of these houses and later archaeological excavations revealed the best preserved prehistoric village in northern Europe, now known as Skara Brae. But whether the events that led to this ancient settlement being abandoned were quite as catastrophic as the woman's beads imply may be open to question.

Skara Brae is vulnerable to sand blow as it lies on a flat grassy plain just above the beach. This type of landscape is called machair, and is peculiar to northwest Britain. Jarlshof in Shetland, Bosta in Lewis, Northton in Harris, Oronsay off Colonsay, numerous sites recently excavated in South Uist and many other west coast prehistoric settlements are all in similar locations.

Skara Brae, Orkney

What is Machair?

The word 'machair' is Gaelic, meaning an extensive, low-lying fertile plain. Gaelic is not native to Orkney and Shetland but elsewhere 'machair' features in placenames, such as Machrihanish in Kintyre, Machair Bay in Islay, Magheramore and Maghera Strand in Ireland, and in places in the Outer Hebrides. 'Machair' has now become a recognised scientific term for a specific coastal feature, defined by some as a type of dune pasture (often calcareous) that is subject to local cultivation, and has developed in wet and windy conditions. This rather restricts the term to the grassy plain alone. Other authorities prefer to consider the whole system, from the beach to where the sand encroaches on to peat further inland; this is the definition used here.

Machair is one of the rarest habitats in Europe, found only in the north and west of Britain and Ireland. Almost half of the Scottish machair occurs in the Outer Hebrides, with the best and most extensive in the Uists and Barra, and also Tiree. Machair sand has a high shell content, sometimes 80 or 90%. This helps distinguish it from the 'links' of eastern coasts, which are formed from more mineral-based sand.

Balranald and Hougharry, North Uist

2

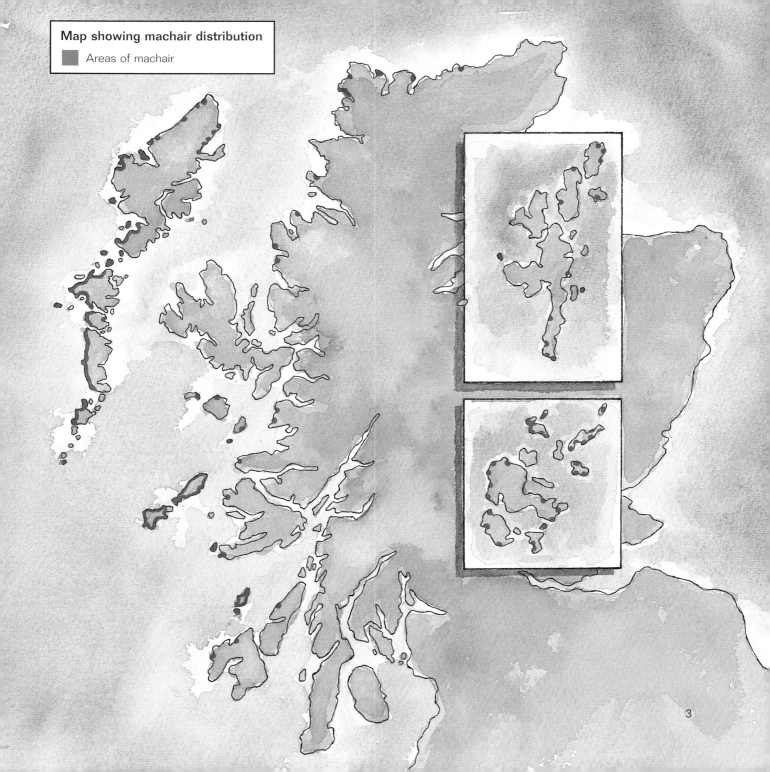

Map showing machair distribution

Areas of machair

3

Seilebost, Harris

How Machair is formed

The generally received theory of the formation
of drift sands and hillocks or downs is this:
the fragments of the shells of molluscous
animals inhabiting the sea near the coasts, are
rolled by the waves toward the shore, where
they are further broken and comminuted. . .
The wind then blows them beyond water-mark,
where, in progress of time, hillocks are
formed. These hillocks are occasionally
broken up by the winds, and blown inland,
covering the fields and pastures. . .

William Macgillivray (1830)

William Macgillivray, who spent much of his youth on the machairs of Northton in Harris, became Professor of Natural History at Aberdeen University. Today scientists might view his remarks as a little simplistic but he is not too far off the mark.

At the end of the last Ice Age, meltwater from the glaciers swept vast amounts of sand and gravel into the sea. The oceans were lower and so the debris was spread over much of what is now the continental shelf. As the sea level rose the glacial sediment - mixed with the crushed shells of masses of molluscs and other marine creatures - were driven ashore by wind and wave action to form characteristic white beaches and coastal sand dunes. The prevailing southwest winds continued to wear away and rebuild the dunes, blowing the light shelly sand over grasslands, marshes and lochs, even reaching the peatland and rocks further inland.

Cross-section of Machair

Moorland with peat lochs

'Blackland' with blown sand overlying peat

Machair plain with lochs, marshes, pasture and cultivation

Coastal dunes with marram

Beach

Sea

Rock

Peat

Calcareous sand

Shell sand components, including limpets and sea urchins

Blowing sand, Tràigh Iar, near Hougharry, North Uist

5

Marram grass, Lingay Strand,
Newton, North Uist
Sea-rocket, Tràigh Iar, near
Hougharry, North Uist

Marram

> [Marram] is the natural inmate of a sandy soil, to which, in fact, it is peculiar. It is therefore obviously the best that could be selected for the purpose of fixing loose sands.
> **William Macgillivray (1830)**

The strandline, highly exposed to wind and wave action, is virtually bare, mobile sand. Only hardy plants like the fleshy-leaved sea rocket and sea sandwort are able to survive. Just above the high-tide mark, where young marram grass begins to take hold, small foredunes begin to develop. With spiky, inwardly-rolled leaves, this grass has a remarkable ability to withstand dry conditions. It thrives upon wind-blown sand and even requires strong winds to break open the seed heads. Its tussocks and deep roots encourage sand to build up and help stabilise the dunes.

Behind such dunes, some up to 10 metres in height, the effects of winds and salt spray are reduced so more plants are able to grow in the bare sand among the marram. Decaying plants hold more moisture and, with less shelly sand being deposited, the soil becomes a little more acid. Marram finally gives way to red fescue and other grasses, mixed in with sand sedge, buttercups, and lady's bedstraw, all of which can still tolerate a thin covering of wind-blown sand in winter.

Sea bindweed

On Ben Eoligarry, Barra, where the sand is blown 100 metres up the rocky slopes inland, there is an unusually abundant covering of primroses.

Sea bindweed has a curious distribution in the Hebrides. It is said to have been introduced by Bonnie Prince Charlie since it grows above the very beach in Eriskay where he stepped ashore in 1745. Somewhat inconveniently, however, it is also recorded from Vatersay, and South Ronaldsay in Orkney; places the Prince never visited!

Winter

Natural influences

'In winter, and even until the middle of May, the western division or machair, is almost a desolate waste of sand'
James Macdonald (1811)

Over the last 8,000 years or so, sand blow has been vital in maintaining the machair landscape and many of its characteristic plants. Blowouts and severe erosion can, however, occasionally be catastrophic and Skara Brae vividly demonstrates how dynamic the landscape can be. Even in recent times changes in sea level and climate, or inappropriate land use, can damage the plants that bind the machair, triggering further sand movement.

Sand and storms

On 19th February 1749, the Reverend John Walker recorded how a hurricane from the northwest, coinciding with high tides, breached an isthmus in Barra, undoubtedly Eoligarry where the airport building now stands. It nearly happened again in 1816.

In 1756 the houses of Baleshare in North Uist were buried in sand up to their roofs. Indeed the name 'Baile sear' means the eastern town, which implies that there would have been a western town 'Baile siar'. The village of Hussaboste is mentioned in a document dated 1389 and was said to have been washed away in the 15th century. It is remembered locally as an offshore reef just west of Baleshare called Sgeir Husabost, while local tradition maintains how it was once possible to journey across to Heisgeir (the Monach Isles) by horse and cart.

In the winter months large areas of the machair can be flooded, protecting it from wind erosion and also providing good feeding grounds for wildfowl. The machair lochs are rich in nutrients and support an interesting range of water plants (including the rare slender naiad), many invertebrates and large numbers of wintering and breeding waterfowl.

Most machair has formed where it is exposed to the full force of Atlantic storms. Just offshore, dense forests of the seaweed, kelp or *Laminaria* help break up the force of the waves. Every winter huge quantities of battered and broken kelp (often referred to as tangle) are thrown up by the waves and form a natural sea wall along the dune edge. The soft, sandy machair shorelines therefore gain essential protection from this stout leathery seaweed - both living and dead.

Seaweed tangle, Lub Bhan, Benbecula

Human influences

It must not be imagined that this Hebridean sand is on a barren soil, it being destitute of vegetation only when drifting loose. When in some degree fixed by moisture, or the interspersion of pebbles and shells, it affords excellent crops of barley, when manured with sea-weeds, and its natural pastures are by far the best.
William Macgillivray (1830)

The rich machair grassland behind the dunes appealed to prehistoric settlers. The inhabitants of Skara Brae were Neolithic farmers; sheep and cattle bones have been unearthed from their middens along with the remains of barley. The light sandy soils were easily tilled and ploughmarks have been uncovered in machair, such as near a Neolithic settlement in Westray. These early ploughs would have scratched the surface rather than turn a furrow and it is likely that these early farmers used seaweed as fertiliser.

The machair is still farmed to this day and although agricultural methods have obviously progressed considerably, seaweed is still a vital component. The application of cast tangle before ploughing adds important organic matter to machair soil that not only enriches it but helps to bind it together, hold moisture and resist wind erosion. It is also vital to the long-term stability of the machair pastures. In much the same way, dung from stock, especially cattle, being wintered out on the open machair, helps humus to form.

The kelp boom

Mrs Angus Campbell bringing seaweed to spread on the fields - South Uist c1930

The harvesting and collection of seaweed occurred extensively during the late eighteenth - early nineteenth centuries. The seaweed was burnt to produce a high quality soda ash that could then be used in the manufacture of glass, soap, bleaching agents and gunpowder. During the Napoleonic wars prices peaked at around £25 a ton. Where Clanranald earned only £5,297 per annum in rent from his South Uist tenants, he was making nearly twice that from his kelping enterprise.

Crofters spent more time processing kelp than tending their fields, diverting seaweed from the land to maximise their income. The population of South Uist increased by 200% during the kelp boom, and in Tiree rose from 1509 to 4391! In 1811 James Macdonald reported how 'the Uists have in many places lost up to one quarter of a mile in breadth by sand drift and sea encroachment'. Exploitation of kelp was exposing the machair to excessive erosion.

Spring

Corn marigolds, South Uist

While May is often the sunniest month in the north and west, it can be dominated by cold easterly winds, so spring comes late to the machair. Dune grassland or links, on the east and south coasts of the mainland, might support hundreds of different plants, yet machair - so much further north - has rather fewer. Nonetheless, a typical patch of machair can look surprisingly rich, with up to 45 species in any metre square. Once the pasture blooms, it presents an astonishing riot of colour for which the machair is justly famous. It is this beauty that draws many tourists to the Northern and Western Isles each summer and inspired generations of Gaelic bards.

11

Sa mhadainn shamhraidh nuair chinneas seamrag,
`S i geal is dearg air a`mhachair chomhnard.
Is lurach, blathmhor a lusan sgiamhach,
Fo dhriuchd na h-iarmailt `s a`ghrian gan oradh.

On a summer morning when the clover burgeons
Red and white on the level machair,
Lovely the plants with their many blossoms,
Fresh with the dew and shining in the sun.

Oran nam Priosanach
by John Maclean (c1886), Tiree

Irish lady's tresses

Early in the season daisies dust the machair like snow but, in places, they can be a sign of heavy grazing. Other white flowers are eyebrights and wild carrot, with cotton grass in wet areas. In June, yellow is the dominant colour, from buttercups, vetches and bird's foot trefoil. On damper ground, silverweed, yellow rattle, and marsh marigolds thrive. Orkney machair has the rare limestone bedstraw. Red and purple become the main colours later in the summer; red clover and ragged robin, with self heal in damp grassland, while field scabious and autumn gentian are unusually common.

Orchids are particular machair highlights. The rare pyramidal and fragrant orchids both occur in the Outer Hebrides. There is a particular Hebridean type of spotted orchid while a small stretch of North Uist has its own variety of marsh orchid, *Dactylorhiza majalis scotica*, found nowhere else. Irish machair can boast bee orchids, its own variety of marsh orchid and the dense-flowered orchid from the Mediterranean.

There are fewer plants where machair meets moorland, on the so-called 'blackland', and here the croft buildings, enriched pasture and hay meadows are found. On Coll and Barra, however, small patches of damp, peaty pasture or marsh grazed by cattle are home to one of the rarest orchids in Europe; Irish lady's tresses. It is mainly a North American species and how it came to colonise the remote western coasts of Scotland and Ireland is still being debated. One theory is that the tiny seeds were transported on the muddy feet of migrant wildfowl such as white-fronted geese.

Wildflowers, Links of
Sumburgh, Shetland

Yellow rattle

Self heal

Machair, Stilligarry,
South Uist

Cultivation

. . . these sands produce crops of barley, oats, rye and potatoes, or of natural grass and wild clover, far beyond what a stranger would expect. They then assume a variegated and beautiful dress, scarcely yielding in colours or perfume to any fields in the kingdom; and being of great extent, they afford a prospect of riches and plenty equalled by no other of the Western Isles.

James Macdonald (1811)

It may be the presence of stock that encourages plants such as orchids, but the real display of machair flowers is greatly enhanced by another agricultural activity; cultivation. This requires the control of grazing; township regulations, on the Uist machair for instance, ask for stock to be removed from unfenced areas by early May. With Uist machair often flooded in wet winters ploughing cannot begin much earlier, yet the sandy soils do dry off quickly.

Horse-drawn or cockshutt ploughs do not dig as deep as modern machines, reducing the risk of wind erosion and helping seeds to germinate. Management recommended by Environmentally Sensitive Area (ESA) schemes insist that crofters complete sowing and harrowing by mid-May, in order not to destroy the early clutches of oystercatchers and ringed plover that like to nest on bare ground exposed by the plough.

14   Cattle on machair, Balemartine, Tiree   Ploughing, Kilkenneth, Tiree

Tiree machair (nearly half of the island's area) is not normally cropped; perhaps because the crofting area further inland is fertile and less rocky, and so more easily ploughed. Cultivation has all but ceased in Barra, Harris and Lewis but it is a requirement of any crofter entering the Uists ESA that 15% or more of the machair share is cropped. Traditionally the area was cultivated on a 2 or 3 year rotation so that no more than half the arable machair will come under the plough at any one time.

With generous amounts of seaweed (the ESA recommends 40 tonnes per hectare), lime-rich machair soils are relatively productive yet they can be rather low in some essential nutrients and trace elements such as copper, cobalt and manganese. In the past livestock were able to make up some of this deficiency while grazing on the hills in summer, but now the animals tend to be kept in fenced areas around the croft so mineral supplements may be required.

Nutrients wash out easily from sandy soils, so artificial fertilisers tend to be ineffective; this limits the crops that can be grown. Only the older strains of small oats and rye will thrive, the latter coping particularly well with the dry conditions as it has strong stalks that resist the wind. Small oats grow quite well in competition with wild flowers which - if the crop is intended as anything other than cattle fodder - would otherwise be condemned as weeds. It is, therefore, not practical to consider expensive herbicide treatment. Early in the season, cereal crops are dominated by corn marigold or charlock, with bugloss, field pansy and cornsalad.

In the first year of fallow, wild pansy, poppies, creeping buttercup and storksbill can flower, clover and red fescue coming through in the second year.

Kilpheder, South Uist

Summer

Machair, Barra

. . . About the first of June when the cattle
are put upon it, it is all over as white as a
cloth, with daisies, and white clover. In that
season, there may be seen pasturing upon it
at once, about 1000 black cattle, 2000 sheep
and 300 horses intermixed with immense
flocks of lapwings and green plovers.
Reverend Dr John Walker (1764)

The Atlantic shores of the Highlands and Islands are a patchwork of beaches, sand dunes, grassland, croftland, wetlands and lochs. Such a range of opportunities for wildlife is so much more enhanced by the way the people manage the land. Rotating the cultivation of the machair year by year provides regular opportunities for annual plants to seed and re-establish. This helps create the spectacular displays of flowers for which the machair is well known. Tiree alone can boast over 500 species of wild plants.

Cultivated machair also has greater numbers and variety of invertebrates. Earthworms, snails, grasshoppers, flies, spiders and harvestmen are all numerous on machair but there are relatively few butterflies and moths; meadow brown, common blues and small tortoiseshell butterflies are most common with dark arches and common rustic being the most widespread moths. The belted beauty is an interesting machair moth - the females being flightless - and one theory is that they might have reached offshore islands on rafts of dead wood. Various bumble bees, including one or two Hebridean specialities, are common over machair grassland.

Belted beauty moth

Birds

Corncrake

The Hebrides have become the last British stronghold of the corncrake with most occurring in Lewis, the Uists and Barra, and Tiree. Long ago people believed corncrakes spent the winter under the ice but we now know that, in May, they arrive from Africa. Rarely seen but characteristically noisy, they seek early cover in iris beds until the hayfields grow tall enough. Although special measures are included for them in the ESAs of the Uists, Shetland and the Argyll Islands, corncrakes tend to be birds of the croftland and hay meadows more than machair grassland and crops.

17

Corn buntings still thrive on cultivated machair in the Uists and Tiree, but are on the verge of extinction on mainland farms. Twite is another characteristic bird of the machair, replacing the linnet found elsewhere, while the rare little tern often forsakes the foreshore to nest on the cultivated land.

Undoubtedly, machair is most famous for its waders. Over 25,000 pairs bred each year on machair during the 1980s, some 6,000 in Tiree alone, with over 17,000 in the Uists and Barra. The other machair areas, in Orkney, Shetland and on the Irish or Scottish mainland, are less rich. The most numerous wader is the peewit or lapwing, a bird now increasingly rare on intensive farmland on the mainland. In the Uists, lapwing breed in the highest densities among the dune slacks and on drier grasslands (up to 85 pairs per km^2). There are fewer in damp machair and fewest on dry cultivated machair and croftland; in Tiree lapwing densities are lower still.

Lapwing

Dunlin are more specific in their breeding requirements preferring the tufted vegetation of wet machair to conceal their nests. A record density of some 300 pairs per km^2 was recorded from one area of South Uist in the 1980s, when some 40% of the British population were to be found on the machairs of the Uists and Tiree alone.

Redshank and snipe prefer the taller vegetation of marshes and wetlands but since the latter tend to be pretty secretive their numbers are likely to have been underestimated. With longer beaks, redshank and snipe (together with dunlin) can probe deeper into wet ground to find food.

It is the oystercatcher and ringed plover that are most dependent upon crofting practices. Both will nest on dry cultivated machair and up to 400 pairs per km^2 of ringed plover have been recorded on ploughed land or recent fallow in the Uists; all together amounting to nearly one-third of the total breeding population in Britain. Ringed plover will also nest on shingle beaches or bare ground, where their camouflaged eggs are best concealed; they also like the broken runways on The Reef in Tiree.

Twite

Dunlin

Redshank

Ringed plover

Autumn

'The crops in North Uist and Benbecula, but especially South Uist, are exposed to a very singular misfortune; being sometimes entirely destroyed by the vast flocks of wild geese, which haunt these islands. This bird is never seen in the south of Scotland except in winter but in these islands it hatches and resides all the year round. . .'

Reverend Dr John Walker (1764)

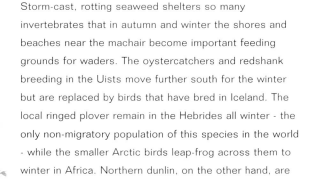

Storm-cast, rotting seaweed shelters so many invertebrates that in autumn and winter the shores and beaches near the machair become important feeding grounds for waders. The oystercatchers and redshank breeding in the Uists move further south for the winter but are replaced by birds that have bred in Iceland. The local ringed plover remain in the Hebrides all winter - the only non-migratory population of this species in the world - while the smaller Arctic birds leap-frog across them to winter in Africa. Northern dunlin, on the other hand, are

20% larger than local dunlin, so birds from Greenland take over for the winter forcing the Hebridean ones to move further south. Turnstones from Greenland and Arctic Canada also overwinter in the Hebrides. Whimbrel, sanderling and purple sandpiper come from Iceland; bar-tailed godwit and grey plover from Siberia. Golden plover are abundant too, some of which breed locally. We do not know if local snipe stay for the winter but with so many taken by estate shooting parties their numbers must be topped up with migrants from further north.

Now that scythes have been replaced by modern machinery, crofters are encouraged - by ESA payments - to delay cutting their hay until August, and to cut from the centre of the field outwards, so that corncrakes can escape from the mower blades into neighbouring crops. The corn is cut in September or early October, having allowed the wild flowers to set seed. Where the fields are too small for binders or balers, the corn may still be tied in sheaves, then stooked before being taken back to the stack yard to be used as winter fodder; some will be threshed as seed for next season.

Later in October, barnacle and white-fronted geese arrive from Greenland, with whooper swans from Iceland. These wildfowl, along with the resident greylag geese, like to feed on the stubble. Recently, the barnacle geese tend to have forsaken some undisturbed offshore islands to frequent improved pasture. Their name derives from an ancient belief that they spent the summer as goose barnacles; stalked, marine crustaceans that look not dissimilar, although very much smaller, of course. Indeed, the Gaelic name for the geese and the barnacles is the same; 'giodhran'.

Barnacle geese

Greylag geese

Greylag geese now breed in several parts of northern Scotland and the Inner Hebrides. There has always been a resident population of birds in the Uists which are reckoned to be the original pure, native stock.

Recent counts indicate about 100 greylags on Colonsay, some 700 on Coll with a similar number on Lewis and Harris, 2,000 on Tiree and about 3,000 on the Uists. Although wildfowlers are permitted to shoot them in winter, the goose numbers are increasing slightly each year. These flocks do not compare with the huge numbers wintering on the mainland and on Islay but, in a crofting context, the damage they might do can still be significant. In some parts of the Uists, for instance, geese can deprive sheep of the first flush of grass on some reseeded pastures in spring, or might flatten or graze ripening corn just prior to harvest in the autumn.

Since cultivation is so important to the conservation interests of machair, geese cannot be allowed to threaten its continuation. In the Uists, a Goose Management Committee has been formed, bringing together crofters, estates, the local council and agencies like the Scottish Office Agriculture, Environment and Fisheries Department (SOAEFD) and Scottish Natural Heritage. Not only does this committee organise regular counts but it assesses complaints and lends out goose scarers. Their role is to minimise pressure on crofting while still retaining a viable breeding population of pure-bred Scottish greylags. A similar committee has now been formed in Tiree.

Greylag goose

Keeping the balance

In summer the cows and milk sheep are sent to the glens, which are covered with heath and hard grasses, sedges and rushes, because the part consisting of soft grass is not in general sufficient for their maintenance during the whole year . . . Black cattle are small but well-shaped. They are covered with a thick and long pile to enable them to resist the winter's cold - a good pile is considered one of the best qualifications of a cow
William Macgillivray's diaries (1818)

Low-intensity land use as practised on the machair is as important for plants and animals as it is to the local people. This distinctive mix of culture, landscape and wildlife generates tourism; so good crofting and nature conservation are a highly viable combination and both are essential to the economy of the islands.

Sheep grazing on Kilpheder machair, South Uist

Golf Course, Scarista machair, Harris

Cattle have long been an important part of the machair system. They do not graze as closely as sheep, taking not only the less appetizing species but also the less attractive portions; more stem, seed heads, dead vegetable material, rushes, cotton grass and other less tasty plants. Cattle, therefore, improve the quality of the grassland for other grazers as well as for wildlife.

In addition, cattle play a part in shaping the machair landscape. Tussocks, for example, are good habitats for invertebrates and thus provide both food and nest sites for birds. Waders have been known to use hoof prints as nest-cups, while some ringed plovers try to conceal their nest beside a dry cow pat. The break-up of coarse plants (such as iris root systems) further opens up and improves the pasture, with any bare patches created being good for invertebrates and as seed beds for annual plants. Dung contains the seeds and grain necessary to regenerate the ground while also adding nutrients and humus.

23

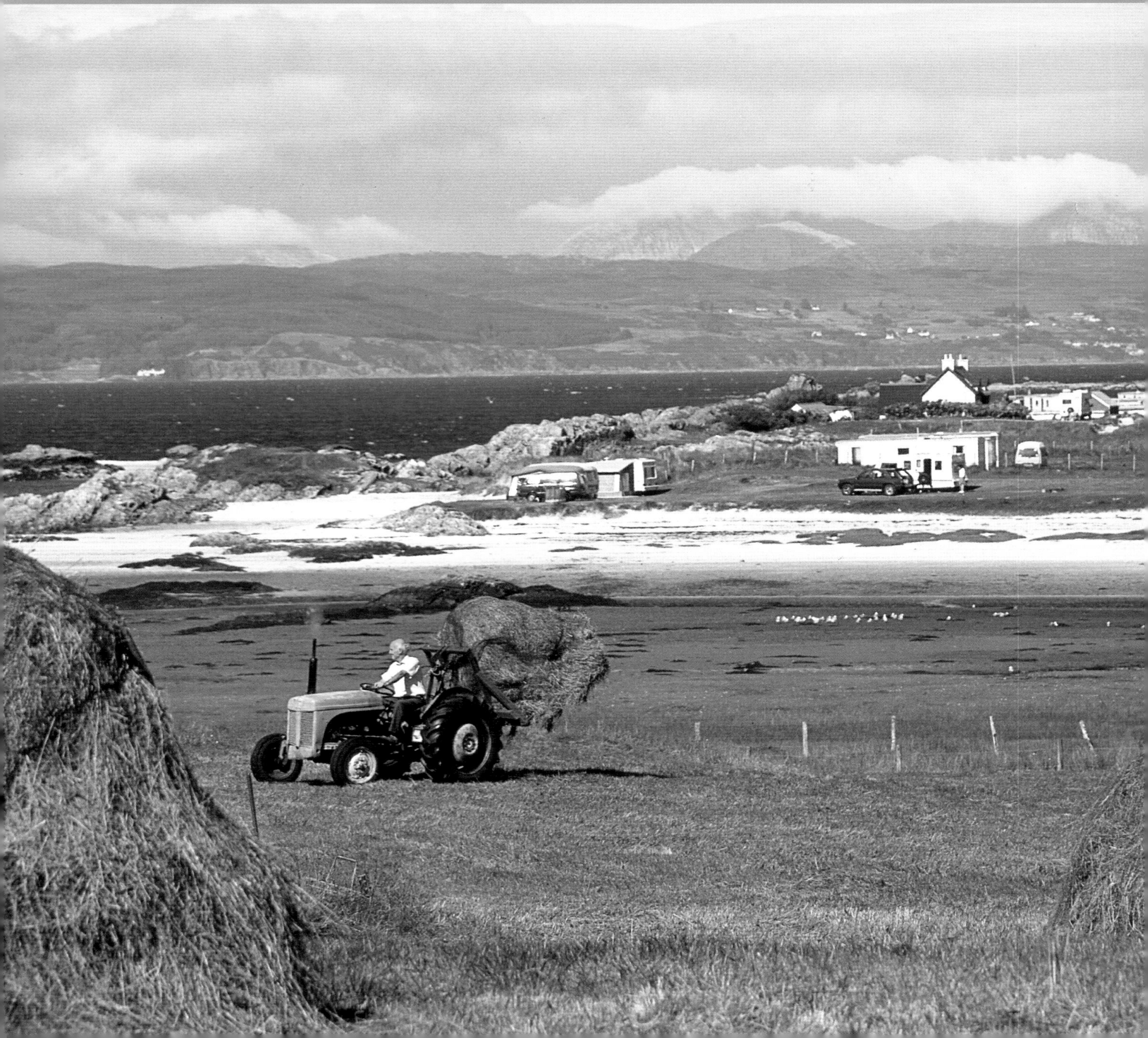
Crofting, Arisaig, Inverness-shire

Too much bare ground eroded (or poached) by stock can, however, encourage invasive weeds, such as ragwort. Sheep will eat this when it is young whereas cattle find it poisonous. While more environmentally-friendly than large numbers of sheep, cattle are quite labour-intensive. It may be the cheapest option to grow winter fodder on the machair, but cattle still need to be fed daily in the winter and even housed in bad weather. If not enough fodder is grown locally feed would have to be bought in, or the cattle even sent off to overwinter on the mainland. This loss of cropped land and of winter dung from the ground is detrimental to any good machair system. Artificial fertilisers reduce the variety of plants and tend to favour the more aggressive, but not necessarily the best, species in the grassland.

Too many sheep can break open the thin dry soils, or rub against sand banks, thus promoting erosion. An unfortunate trend in recent years has been to fence off individual apportionments of machair to confine stock all the year round. This leads to heavy grazing in summer preventing plants from flowering or setting seed and leading to less variety of species. It also removes cover for nesting and feeding birds and increases the risk of nests being trampled.

Agricultural support should be geared to helping crofters continue their already environmentally-friendly practises. Environmentally Sensitive Area schemes provide one such opportunity, where special payments promote cropping the machair, applying seaweed or dung, employing measures that favour grassland birds and managing wetlands sympathetically. There is even support for townships to construct sand-blow fencing and to plant marram against erosion.

Oldshore Beg, Sutherland

Alien introductions

The mammals that have naturally colonised the Northern Isles, the Inner and Outer Hebrides are limited; pygmy shrews, field voles, Orkney vole, mice and rats, otters, red deer and seals. It is probably the absence of land predators, including foxes and stoats, that has resulted in such high numbers of ground-nesting birds, such as waders and corncrakes. Feral cats can be a nuisance, as can a more recent introduction, ferrets. They were originally brought to the island to control the rabbits, themselves imported by humans, as a potential source of food. Tiree and Berneray (off North Uist) still have no rabbits although the latter will be at risk of invasion over the new causeway.

Hedgehog

Rabbit damage on machair

There is no justification for introducing any wild animal to an island. Ferrets have never succeeded in controlling rabbits. Rats and cats (and mink in Lewis and Harris) have wiped out many bird colonies. Hedgehogs - introduced to the Uists in the 1970s - are not munching the garden slugs as was expected, but instead find waders' eggs more appealing. Recent studies by SNH and the Royal Society for the Protection of Birds have shown a serious drop in wader numbers in South Uist and Benbecula, while North Uist too is now being invaded by this prickly predator; they are also present in Coll and Tiree.

The future

Many examples of machair have been designated Sites of Special Scientific Interest, Special Protection Areas or Special Areas of Conservation (under the European Directives) or as nature reserves. This helps promote appropriate management for the benefit of wildlife. But there are more major problems. With global warming adding to a gradual rise in sea level and an increase in Atlantic storms, the threat of erosion is greater than ever. Rabbits, and stock, can add to dune erosion, while dumping of rubbish, uncontrolled vehicle/caravan access to machair and dune buggies or motorbikes tearing up sand slopes can create local problems. Yet still, there are few beaches more lovely and unspoilt than those of the Northern and Western Isles; all very important for the local tourist trade (though perhaps midges, cool winds and cold seas help make sure they never become over popular!)

Rubbish dumping on machair

Sand dunes, Luskentyre, Harris

Marram should never be abused. It should be cut only for thatching, or for transplanting in dune stabilisation works, within strict guidelines, in moderation and well back from any actively-eroding edge. Every opportunity should be taken to prevent blow-outs, and any replanting should be undertaken as sensitively as possible. Marram is always a better solution than unsightly, less effective and expensive, man-made defences.

Left over from the Ice Age, shingle beaches form a vital defence from eroding waves. The preservation of this natural barrier is very important and it should only be interfered with in exceptional circumstances; and certainly not for commercial uses. Kelp beds are another important protection so any offshore exploitation by the seaweed industry should be discouraged, The winter cast of tangle not only provides vital protection against storms but is also essential to the maintenance of the machair and traditional land use.

Machair is a unique and dynamic habitat. It is one of the best examples of a distinctive culture with a finely-tuned land use successfully supporting an extremely rich wildlife resource. Generations of local folk have understood enough of the system to use it to their advantage, to cherish it for their very survival and to pass on this knowledge to their children. But pressures of modern living threaten to undermine that ancient balance. We still need to have a better understanding of machair and its wildlife in order that the needs of the people living there can be provided for, since machair without people would be a very much poorer place. In accepting that sand blow will always be a necessary feature of life on the Atlantic fringe, we need to be aware of the most effective ways to contain it so that the experience of Skara Brae's deserted village may remain a feature of prehistory.

I can't think of a single bo▓ in the same way as *Leavi▓* filled with grace, gospel pointing the reader aw▓ ▓g▓▓▓▓ ▓▓▓▓ following and back to Jesus. Thank God for Kendra's heart to help those on their journey from the burdensome life of legalism to the life-giving freedom of the cross. Jesus really is enough!

—Kimm Crandall
Author of Beloved Mess and **Christ in the Chaos**

Kendra doesn't just write from the heart, she writes from experience, and both spill out of the pages of *Leaving Legalism*. This book is filled with Kendra's heart's desire to see people freed from legalism and religiosity and all the damage both do in your life. She knows. She's been there. This book is her way of walking alongside you on the road to leaving legalism and finding real, lasting freedom in Christ.

—Caroline Howard
Certified Life Breakthrough Coach

Leaing Legalism is a book the modern church needs —a grace-filled, heart-nourishing volume you can read in an evening and apply for a lifetime. Kendra hits the balance perfectly, helping readers to shed the burden of legalism, stop trying to earn forgiveness, and learn to walk again as the children of a trusted and loving heavenly father.

—Hal & Melanie Young
Authors of **Raising Real Men**

Out of her own pain and personal journey, Kendra has written a heart-felt book that reads like a primer for leaving legalism in the past and embracing the pure gospel. It proves enormously helpful for anyone walking away from spiritual abuse and pain. Start your journey to healing here!

—Jessica Thompson
Author of **Mom, Dad, What's Sex?**

LEAVING LEGALISM

————————————————

Learning to Love God, Others, and Yourself
Again

With Resources and Questions for
Reflection and Discussion

KENDRA FLETCHER

Copyright © 2018 by Kendra Fletcher

Dreamy (5x8) Self-Publishing Template © 2017 Renee Fisher
https://www.reneefisher.com

Cover Design: Jen Flora
Cover Photo: Lightstock
Pendulum Graphic: Jayne Fletcher

ISBN-13: 9781720020141

Dedication

To Redeemer Modesto,
where we landed in need of healing. You got
out of the way so we could see Jesus.

To Jim, who preached the words that pointed
us to freedom in Christ. Forever grateful, my
friend.

Table of Contents

Introduction

And worse, there is a crack in everything that you can put together: physical objects, mental objects, constructions of any kind. But that's where the light gets in, and that's where the resurrection is and that's where the return, that's where the repentance is. It is with the confrontation, with the brokenness of things.
-Leonard Cohen

One of the most difficult things about being a former and recovering member of a legalistic church, a cult-like community, or a bonafide cult, is the response we get from people who didn't know us when we were a part of those communities and who learn our stories after the fact. Many are incredulous, and they seem to doubt what we are telling them.

"What? Really? That seems so crazy!"

And yes, it is. But harder than responding to their disbelief is the fact that most of us simply feel foolish. A response of incredulity always makes me feel as if the other person thinks I must be a moron; I mean, how can an otherwise seemingly intelligent adult fall prey to such extremism?

I haven't done an extensive period of research into the psychology of why and how people join legalistic communities, but I know this: It likely isn't their intelligence that is driving their choices.

More often than not, it is a felt need that makes us join in, whether slowly like the proverbial frog in the kettle, or a quick noisy splash straight into the deep-end. For us, it was a progression driven by our fear and pride.

Parenting lit a fire underneath us that caused us to stop focusing on the source of our hope (God) and start looking around for methods and theories and promises to feed our fears. If you've ever parented anyone, you likely understand the fear. Add to our anxiety that we were going to royally mess up our kids was our pride; we were going to do it right, and we didn't need anyone else's help. Thank you very much.

It might not have been parenting that drove you to embrace a legalistic church or community. I'm betting between the two of us, we could come up with a thousand other catalysts that combine to create the perfect storm in the life of someone who finds her or himself eventually the victim of the spiritual abuse that invariably accompanies such environments. Whatever the reason, you are here now, reading, searching, hurting.

Me too. But I have a hope that spurs me to

believe that there is healing for even the deepest recesses of our pain. Have you lost that hope? Leaving legalism is a watershed event that can either cause us to run as far and fast from Christ and his followers as possible, or drive us right into the sheltering, loving, merciful, accepting arms of the One who created us to be free.

I believe, wholeheartedly, that we can heal. I believe that we can learn, once again, to love God, others, and yes, even ourselves. That's the beautiful conclusion to leaving legalism.

-Kendra

*Each story told in *Leaving Legalism* is a composite, or, except in the case of Royal Robbins, names and locations have been changed in order to protect identities.

Chapter 1 – How We Became Homeschool Legalists
(Yes, That's a Thing)

I never wanted to homeschool. In fact, when we began even considering homeschooling, we didn't actually know any kids who had been homeschooled all the way through. All we had to go on was a friendly and vivacious high school girl we'd known in college when we were volunteers in her youth group and a few families with elementary-aged kids. But then, we weren't in it for the long haul, so it didn't matter what the outcome was other than giving our kids a solid couple of early years around our kitchen table.

We married on a hot July afternoon in 1991, right between my junior and senior year of college, and then we packed up our meager post-university belongings and moved to San Francisco so my husband Fletch could begin three years of a year-around dental school program while I worked to pay the rent on our 600 square-foot apartment above the pizza parlor. Two weeks later, I found myself throwing up during my lunch break and surrendering the making of dinner to my student husband; the sight of a can of corn sent me reeling to the toilet.

The lady at the free clinic seemed bored and disinterested when she confirmed my suspicions. I was due in March, and did I want to keep the baby? No question. My conservative Christian upbringing had surrounded me with capable mothers and I had always wanted to be one.

I worked, we welcomed our firstborn son, then a second. My husband eventually graduated, emerging from a daunting dental school workload accompanied by back-to-back bottles of Pepto Bismol to fight the stress and pressure of school, and then the delegation of DDS on his diploma.

We moved out of the city into suburbia.

I'm convinced that God has a great big sense of humor, because while I flippantly declared in all my 20-something wisdom that I was too selfish to homeschool my kids, I began to meet them: the homeschoolers.

Surprisingly, they weren't weird. There in the multi-programmed mega church of the 90's, I saw these women so committed to their kids, and they were strong, gutsy, and vocal. They talked of pouring into their kids, of spending the best hours of the day with them, of walking alongside them in the spirit of Deuteronomy 11:19. It was good mothering, and their homes were mostly warm and friendly.

We had this four-year-old pistol of a boy, too, and he made me wonder at his academic future. I wanted so badly to put him into kindergarten, but something held me back. His tenacity and general lack of self control were not a good combination for a classroom setting; I was sure he would quickly become bored and then find himself sitting in the principal's office.

I reluctantly stuck my toe into homeschooling waters. I pursued experienced homeschoolers. Sitting at Catherine's kitchen table, I soaked up all her knowledge and watched as her kids seemed to like being home. They squabbled, mostly under their collective breath, but they weren't nerds and they weren't copping a teenage attitude, either. It was good, and I wanted a home like that.

"I'll homeschool him for preschool", I declared one Sunday afternoon as we drove home from church. "What do you think?" Fletch has always been the kind of husband who thinks he married the girl-who-can-do-anything, and he nodded in agreement. "I think that would be great!" A little counter-cultural perhaps, but we were both native Californians and comfortable with the unconventional anyway.

That was January. In March, our firstborn turned 5 and by May, he was reading. That precocious, bright, energetic 5-year-old who could already read and craft little legal loopholes in his head became my first kindergarten student, and thus we surrendered to the advantages of one-on-one teaching around our own kitchen table. We had firmly planted our flag in the homeschooling camp, and with it, began a march toward the subtle legalism that would eventually leave us feeling battered and burned out.

———

Maybe your story of how you got involved in a rigid, rule-loving community is like ours. Maybe you stumbled into it because you saw its outward-facing strengths and thought it could solve a problem or fill a void. Or maybe your religious convictions guided your entry into a legalistic view of Christianity, eventually adhering you to a lifestyle that was all-or-nothing. Either way, you found yourself wrapped up in something that defined who you are, what you did, and how you behaved.

The modern homeschool movement has been like that. Fueled by convictions and fed by a growing unease with the failures of the public school institutions in North America (1), parents with a little bit of moxie and a desire to raise their children in the nurture and admonition of the Lord (Ephesians 6) identified themselves as "homeschoolers", and they stuck together in tight clusters because they desired "like-mindedness" with others who had committed to raising their children in the same manner.

When our church decided to model itself after a popular "seeker sensitive" mega church of the mid-'90's, we became uneasy. One Sunday morning the pastor preached a sermon that had a lot more in common with a seminar on health than on the exposition of Scripture, and we counted it as our swan song. It was time to move on, and we found ourselves quietly leaving at the same time as a few other families we knew. In our immaturity, we were staunchly certain that we were right and those we left behind at our former church were wrong, and part of that judgmental viewpoint added homeschooling to the list of how we had gotten it "right".

Faced with having to define what exactly we did believe and granted the luxury of the time to decide, we and three other families began to meet together to study theology and decide where to go next.

Several years later, we eventually came to believe that there simply weren't any churches in our area doing it right, and we needed to start our own. "Right" for us was a particular brand of theology, a singular form of church government, a family-integrated church model like what we had seen beginning to emerge from dynamic speakers such as Doug Phillips (2) and Scott Brown (3), and families who were committed to homeschooling.

We believed that women ought to be home raising children and homeschooling them, dads were the leaders of the homes (with a particular emphasis on patriarchy), children are a blessing and therefore each family should have or adopt as many as God would give, children ought to be in church with mom and dad at all costs, and unmarried adult daughters ought to be home serving their fathers until they had a husband they could turn and serve in his place. I could cover in detail the philosophies behind these beliefs, but in the interest of moving forward through our story, I'll leave it here, noting that this was a prevalent brand of ideology common amongst conservative Christian homeschoolers in the 1990's and 2000's.

I remember during that decade of our lives that I often felt the crushing weight of our adherence to our philosophies, but I couldn't identify why I felt so burdened and I certainly could not admit it to myself or to those with whom we were so "like-minded". There weren't supposed to be any weaknesses in our systems, and if there were cracks, we couldn't safely admit them. The emphasis on outward behavior was so compelling and the judgment so strong for families who chose not to walk lockstep that there was no safety in being transparent. In fact, I was told by another woman during those years that when we show our weaknesses, it isn't edifying to other women in the body of Christ.

And so I trudged on, unable to understand why this Christian life was so void of the joy it promised. I remember driving home one afternoon, one of the few times I found myself alone in my van. I was desperately crying out to God, "You say your yoke is easy and your burden is light, but this doesn't feel easy or light! This feels like a crushing weight I can't carry anymore!"

I didn't make the connection between our own religious behaviorism and my feelings of desperation and despair. It would take nearly losing three of our children to wake us up from our "gospel amnesia"; we had forgotten the freedom given to us through the gospel, and God was about to reacquaint us with himself.

———

In the summer of 2008, I found our 7-week-old baby in a coma. His tiny body lay in the Moses basket where I had put him down to sleep hours before, but his skin was clammy and cold, his eyes were rolled back in his head, and his lips were blue. He was barely breathing.

Our littlest boy, whom we began to call "Mighty Joe" during his ordeal, had contracted an enterovirus, and in the weeks that followed he suffered liver failure, kidney failure, heart damage, and brain damage. We brought him home with no assurance of his future and warnings from specialists that he was probably going to be blind, deaf, and a vegetable. To say that Mighty Joe's life has changed ours would be a hefty understatement.

Six months after bringing our baby boy home to recuperate, I accidentally ran over our 5-year-old with our 12-passenger van. Rounding the circular driveway, she assumed I was parking and jumped out, only to have the back tire go over her completely. In the hours that followed, CPS visited our home and our little girl began what was six weeks of immobility as her fractured pelvis healed.

She was alive and getting stronger each day, but what was my worst nightmare tumbled with forward momentum into the unthinkable: a CPS report. Quickly, both the police officer and the CPS caseworker recognized that this was purely an accident, but our world was thoroughly rocked and there would be no going back to life as we knew it. Thankfully.

Life as we knew it was rule-bound, narrow, and rigid. It camped on outward signs of an inward faith that threw its hope into methods rather than the Savior, into our good choices and works, rather than what Jesus had already accomplished at the cross. As we began to wake up from what we would begin to recognize as "gospel amnesia"— forgetting the simple truths that Jesus carried our sins to the cross and we are now forgiven—we felt push-back from our church body, a family-integrated, homeschool-is-the-best-way community that preached law regularly from the pulpit without the beauty of the gospel at the core.

We would plead with the pastors, "Please, remind us of what Jesus did for us. What has to be done will flow out of that love, but if you keep telling us what we must do, we will be crushed under the weight of the law". We were told Jesus was not enough. The predominant message in the life of our church was that we needed to do more and try harder or God would not be pleased with us.

We wrestled internally. We watched men corner visitors to the church and try to correct their view of eschatology, capturing them in conversations so that the elders and deacons could be certain the visitors were on the same theological page as the rest of us. When I once ventured to ask, "What happens to the family that comes to our church who doesn't homeschool, maybe the wife works, and they think they'd like a Sunday School program for their kids?" I shouldn't have been surprised that the answer was, "We'd try to change them."

Where was Jesus? Buried under the weight of our incomplete view of him, as always happens when we begin to change our focus from the One who redeems our souls to the many and varied gifts and tools he bestows upon us. We so easily shift our hope to our methods, when Jesus and nothing added to Jesus is the only answer.

While we were working through our misguided hope and marveling at the peace and freedom beginning to wash over us as we were moving away from our legalistic community and back toward the cross, we found ourselves in yet another crisis situation with one of our children. One morning on the tail end of a flu that had swept through and interrupted life for everyone in our home, we awoke to find our 8-year-old in septic shock.

We rushed her to the ER where she was prepped for and undergoing emergency surgery in less than an hour. Her appendix had ruptured sometime over the previous 48 hours, hiding itself underneath the stomach flu, and the infection was killing her. Three weeks and two additional surgeries later, we were back home and reeling from yet another near miss with a precious child.

There are permanent ramifications for two of our children. Mighty Joe has brain damage and struggles with visual perception, speech, and auditory processing, and he has trouble making connections because of frontal lobe injury. Caroline, our then-8-year-old with the ruptured appendix, will likely not be able to have children without some sort of medical intervention. We are reminded every day of God's grace and care for us through each child in our home, but especially because of the trials we went through with three of them during that particularly pressing 18-month period of our lives.

Through all of the pain and upheaval, God was speaking. How could we not hear him in the din of such desperation? If you've sat at the bedside of a child whose life hangs in the balance, you understand the profundity of such a life-altering experience. We had waded through three such experiences, and God was just beginning to breathe life once again into our tired and worn-out souls.

Are you there, too? Is your story some variation of ours, where homeschooling or some other otherwise good philosophy or ideology has morphed into a lifestyle that has overtaken your family? (4) Are you deep into a community that lives in judgment, is driven by fear, and struggles to give anyone else the benefit of the doubt? Is it time to move back toward the cross and Jesus' redemptive work there? To find freedom and healing?

I've written this book because I want to help you turn your eyes once again upon Jesus. That day when he hung on the cross at Calvary he said, on your behalf, "It is finished", and he meant finished. All of it. Let's discover together what it means to live under the words that declare that he has paid it all, and there's no amount of homeschooling, homesteading, theological study, church community, or religious behavior that can add to what he's already accomplished.

> That day when he hung on the cross at Calvary he said, on your behalf, "It is finished," and he meant finished. All of it.

(1)Modern homeschooling in other countries has its roots in the 1980's and 1990's, too.

(2)President of the now-defunct Vision Forum Ministries, San Antonio, TX

(3)President of the National Council of Family Integrated Churches, www.ncfic.org

(4) In case you're wondering, we haven't stopped homeschooling. At the time of this book, I'm still homeschooling one son full-time, and two daughters' high school English and history classes. We love homeschooling, but we have learned to put it in its proper place; it is not our hope.

———

On the next page, you'll find some questions for discussion, but I'll be honest with you: I don't usually love reflection questions at the end of chapters. Often they seem as if they were stuck on by a publisher who needed the book to be a bit longer, and they don't seem to really get to the matters of the heart.

My intention in providing these questions at the end of each chapter is so that you can begin to un-peel, as it were, the layers of lies, uncertainty, and inevitable idolatry that have clouded your faith while you were entrenched in a legalistic church.

Take your time. Answer them in a way that works for you: written, read, or discussed with a friend or two.

Questions to Ask Yourself

1. Think through your own journey. What initially led you to the church you eventually needed to leave?

2. What physical/tangible facets of the community drew you to it? (i.e., the community was welcoming, I felt my kids would be safe there, we were "like-minded" in our lifestyle choices, the leadership was dynamic, etc.)

3. What is the acute need that caused you to pick up this book? What are you hoping God will say or do as you begin to wrestle with the consequences of living in legalism?

Chapter 2 – The Pendulum

She lost her parents when she was still too young and found herself growing up in the home of a cold and detached relative that left her feeling like an outsider every day. The weekend she moved into her college dorm, she was dropped off with her suitcases and left with the understanding that she was now entirely on her own.

Looking for someone or something to fill the emptiness she inevitably felt inside, she entered relationship after relationship, hoping that the next guy would be "the one". Her career began to take shape and she hoped that it, too, would bring her a sense of fulfillment and worth. The world had been telling her for the past two-and-a-half decades that she would find happiness in a career and a man, and she believed the rhetoric. Her job brought a sense of accomplishment and became a source of identity, informing her of her self-worth and value.

She met a man at work, and eventually they married in the spring. She settled back into her career. Their first year became sleepy, then increasingly unstable. One day as she was cleaning their bedroom, she discovered a stack of vulgar magazines carelessly stuffed into his nightstand—the filthiest kind of porn—and it devastated her. When she confronted him with her find, he became immediately enraged, screaming that she was worthless, that he had to resort to making love to the images on the glossy printed paper because she was so unfulfilling to him, throwing the magazines at her and leaving her in a stunned and crippled pile on the kitchen floor.

That moment seemed to unlock the true character of the man she had married. Soon she discovered that he also had a drug problem, an addictive personality that immersed itself in alcohol, porn, gambling, and lying to cover it all up.

It didn't help that as he was revealing his depravity, she was finding Jesus. Her despair led her to the little church across the street, and the people there loved her in her fear and despondency.

When their divorce became final, she pressed into the community of believers at her church. It was a gift of new life, a fresh take on the old life of fear and pain, and the longed-for acceptance, simply because of what Jesus had done for her.

She met a man in that group of believers, and after a few careful months of dating, they were married. She hadn't really dealt with the brokenness that marked her childhood and previous marriage, though, and so she entered that marriage with a countenance that craved security. Her new marriage was, essentially, couched in fear, and she began to lean more heavily on her new husband than on her newfound faith in Christ.

When circumstances led to leaving the church where they had met, the new couple's fear, high standards of religious behavior, and the need to get it "right" drove them straight into a rigid church community with specific standards of outward dress and conduct. From appropriate gender roles to child-rearing methods to a distinct brand of theology, they became steeped in and driven by the rules of the community, both spoken and unspoken.

They swung the proverbial pendulum. This movie was allowed but not that one. Their children could read these classics but not those. Dress lengths had to be this long, boy's clothing in this style, Bible reading and church attendance mandatory. Food had to be homemade.

It's so easy for us to do what this young couple did, even if the details aren't exactly the same. We are, in a sense, running from all that formed our prison before we got out of whatever the circumstances were. Some of us are sprinting 180 degrees in the opposite direction from a lifestyle that only brought us destruction.

If there were drugs, we may equate our former addictions with a life out of control, and we now allow nothing that could become an addiction, from coffee to video games.

If there was rock and roll, we equate its sound and atmosphere with a life out of control, and we now allow nothing that smacks of "worldly" rock music.

If there was sexual promiscuity, we equate the emotional wreckage with a life out of control, and we now tell our children that they cannot be alone with anyone of the opposite sex.

Pendulum swinging means we've put our hope in whatever behavior is opposite the prior negative behaviors, rather than in Christ. We feel safe. We feel smart, possibly better than others who don't share our convictions. But our hope-shifting ultimately leads to our own bondage, even if the things we shift our hope to are innocuous. I mean, what's negative about telling our teenagers they're not allowed to date?

Nothing, really, unless we've shifted our hope to our kids not dating as the answer to all of our past sinful choices. If we think that keeping our kids from spending time alone with the opposite sex is the answer to them choosing whether or not to have sex before marriage, we've erected an idol in place of Jesus, and that's the very definition of hope-shifting. (1)

A pendulum swing is visible evidence that we are putting our hope in the choices we make, the things we do, and the things we don't do. Instead of our life and lifestyle choices being an outgrowth of what our true hope, Jesus Christ, has already done for us, we put all of our pebbles in the bucket that tells us, "This thing. This decision. This conviction. All of this will bring you the answers you're looking for." But there is only one healer, and he holds the pebbles. He heals by his own hand and is the singular hope for all of our doubt, fear, pain, and sin.

> He heals by his own hand and is the singular hope for all of our doubt, fear, pain, and sin.

Hear me here: It's not wrong to have rules or standards in place in your home or for your own life, of course. The problem is that, in our humanity, we so badly want to place our hope in something—sometimes anything—and we so often place it in the tools that God has given us rather than in God Himself.

That's huge, isn't it?

All through Scripture we see evidence of people placing their hope in the things God had given, rather than in God:

- Adam and Eve put their hope in a shiny piece of fruit that came with a dicey promise from the ultimate salesman. That apple was going to make them better than they already were. (Genesis 3)
- Cain put his hope in eliminating his brother.

Murder would cover his shame and make God love him more. (Genesis 4)

- The people who settled in Shinar put their hope in a tower they erected. Reaching the heavens with their building would make them closer to God and show their enemies how powerful they were, thus eliminating their need to trust in anyone other than themselves. (Genesis 11)

And just those three stories take us all the whopping way to Genesis 11. Eleven chapters into the Old Testament, and we see three major pendulum-swinging hope-shifting accounts that brought, instead of the longed-for hope, destruction in their wake.

Somewhere in the middle of the pendulum is the truth. The gospel. In fact, right smack dab in the middle of the pendulum, at equilibrium position, is Jesus. The cross. The truth. The way. The life. Can you picture that?

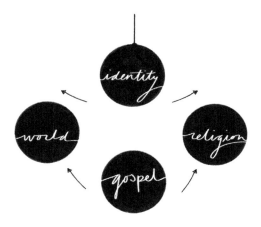

It's a striking reminder that we humans tend toward whatever we think is offering us our best hope in the moment, whether that's a diet promising our dream body (which then promises a whole lot of other things, from relationship security to likeability) or a career position promising more money which, of course, promises financial fulfillment (and probably also relationship security and likeability).

But to those of us who found ourselves drowning in the deep, dark waters of legalism, the trap of pendulum swinging seems even more insidious. If, before our religious adherence and rigidity, we lived a life without restraint that led to a whole lot of pain and personal destruction, we are those people who swing the pendulum over to rule-keeping and law-loving because certainly, some boundaries will be the answer to all of our suffering.

Again, *boundaries are a good thing.* Guardrails are put in place on dangerous stretches of highway for a reason, and it's always for our good. But boundaries, guardrails, rules, laws, right living—*these things are not our hope.* Jesus is our hope, and in his perfection, we are told that he fulfilled all the laws. All of the law.

> Jesus is our hope, and in his perfection, we are told that he fulfilled all the laws. All of the law.

And on the opposite side of the pendulum, pushing back as it were, are those of us who are now leaving legalism, and we toss the rules and the boundaries and the right living over the guardrail to find their death after a quick, vertically soaring dive off the edge.

Where is the healthy response? Where ought we be swinging? Right in the middle, at equilibrium position, where stands the cross and the gospel and our Savior, Jesus Christ. Run from rules and rigid communities and arbitrary standards of dress and behavior, but stand with Jesus. And be patient with yourself. It takes a long time for most of us to stop making broad pendulum swings.

Easier said than done? Stay with me. We'll talk about what it means to separate the legalism from the act of following Jesus without the wild, sweeping swing of the proverbial pendulum.

(1) *Hope-Shifting: Finding our Acceptance, Security, Purpose, Value, and Significance*, Jim Applegate, CreateSpace, 2015

Questions to Ask Yourself

1. Each of us swings the pendulum from time to time. As you look back on your own life, where do you see yourself making wide swings from the gospel to the world and from the gospel to religious behavior?

2. List each pendulum swing you've made individually. (This is painful, I realize, but unless we take the time to examine what got us here, we're not really dealing with the truth in our own hearts and then our healing is stunted or just never happens at all.)

3. Are you willing to allow someone to speak into your life right now and help you see where you might be swinging the pendulum post-legalism?

4. As we leave an environment where we've been told what to do, it may be difficult to let someone else in as a voice of balance, but scripture reminds us of the importance of healthy community for this reason. Can you begin to pray about who God might bring into your life and point you back to Jesus? (It is entirely okay if you're not ready to take this step.)

Chapter 3 – Why Rules Feel Safe

When I was 15 years old, one of the world's most popular musicals hit the Broadway stage and I was undone by its scope, score, music, acting, and depth. *Les Misérables* is, of course, based on the classic Victor Hugo novel written to elucidate the social issues leading up to the French Revolution. That could seem super boring if you're not into French history, but there is a far greater story of redemption woven throughout, beginning with the awakening of our protagonist, Jean Valjean, to his intrinsic value as a man loved by God. Reading *Les Misérables* undid me at 15 and it continues to illuminate the corners of my own gracelessness.

Amongst its many layers of masterful storytelling and character development stands the commanding, sanctimonious adversary of our hero. Javert is the police inspector who becomes, over the course of the novel, obsessed with the pursuit and punishment of Jean Valjean, because when Jean Valjean was a young man in his 20's, he stole a loaf of bread to feed his seven starving nieces and nephews. It was a desperate time, and Valjean served 19 years of hard labor before his release.

But for our purposes, I want us to focus on Inspector Javert. So devoted is Javert to the law that, Hugo writes, "[H]e would have arrested his own father if he escaped from prison and turned in his own mother for breaking parole. And he would have done it with that sort of interior satisfaction that springs from virtue." (1)

In fact, we can say that all of Javert's moral foundation is built strictly on legalism. He loves the law, upholds it, and sees everything by the light of it.

At some point in my initial reading of *Les Misérables* as an enamored 15-year-old, I began to take notes. My battered paperback copy is covered in clear contact paper, dog-eared, highlighted, and underlined. It is curious to me now, as the woman who spent a decade of her life embracing the harsh law-loving religion of a cult-like community, that I had both underlined and highlighted the following passage describing the consummation of a life lived in cold adherence to the law, like Javert's:

"Probity, sincerity, candor, conviction, the idea of duty, are things that, when in error, can turn hideous, but — even though hideous — remain great; their majesty, peculiar to the human conscience, persists in horror. They are virtues with a single vice — error. The pitiless, sincere, joy of a fanatic in an act of atrocity preserves some mournful radiance that inspires veneration. Without suspecting it, Javert, in his dreadful happiness, was pitiful, like every ignorant man in triumph. Nothing could be more poignant and terrible than this face, which revealed what might be called all the evil of good." (2)

". . .all the evil of good."

Here's the long and short of it: When we love the law, our good works, and our Christianity more than we love our Savior, we can be sure that our good has turned to evil. In our "dreadful happiness", we become pitiful.

In the end, Jean Valjean spares the life of Inspector Javert — twice. And now Javert is in tumultuous inner-conflict. The law, which is infallible, has been replaced by something he cannot understand: the grace of God. Javert scurries like a cornered rat through the streets of Paris, struggling with the seemingly antipathetic natures of law and grace, climbs stalwartly onto the ledge overlooking the Seine, and plunges into the icy waters to his death.

We love the law because we think it is the answer.

We love the law because we think it will ease our pain.

We love the law because we think it will keep all

the world's evil in check.

We love the law because all those rules make us feel safe.

We love the law because we think that by keeping it, God will be pleased with us, and if he's pleased with us, he'll give us good things.

For a time, we see that our adherence to the laws of the Old Testament, or our church, or in our own heads, works. The law really does seem to be the answer, because it affects change at the level of what is observable from the exterior of our lives. Our children seem to obey our laws. We may even feel our pain, often stemming from the emotions and turmoil of our past experiences, easing.

And we do see how the law, in general, keeps evil in check. Criminals are convicted, as it should be.

This may come as a surprise, but the law itself is not the problem. In fact, keeping the Ten Commandments is just a good, solid, humane way to live: obey God, respect your parents, don't lie, don't steal, don't kill anyone . . . In addition to being "nice guys" and good citizens, we are often blessed by the results of our good works. We do something good for someone and they do something good in return. We refrain from killing our neighbor and that keeps us out of jail. The law is half of a solid economy whose currency is abiding by the rules.

But what Jesus is more concerned with is the other half of that economic solution: us. Our hearts. Our sin nature and our need for a Savior. His role in our lives. Until new life has been breathed into the people part of the law/people/outcome solution, the

> But Jesus is more concerned with is the other half of that economic solution: us. Our hearts.

law stands as the infallible standard in which we come out the losers every single time. The law either wins by crushing us under the weight of our attempts to uphold it line by line or by our failure to do so.

So why the law, then? And why is Scripture full of praise for its merits? David in particular camped on the law and even wrote songs and psalms in its praise:

"Oh how I love your law! It is my meditation all the day." Psalm 119:97

If we look at the New Testament, where we get to see and hear Christ as a human man, we learn that he is here to fulfill that law (Matthew 5:17-20), and that the law illuminates and illustrates our need for a Savior who gently and thoroughly remakes us into his perfect image. That, in fact, is the purpose of the law. When we begin to wrap our finite brains around all of this, we can make sense of the proper place of the law in our own lives.

For some of us, grace and the proper place of the law in our lives is not understood until we need grace ourselves. When Inspector Javert's understanding of the incompleteness of the law was blown wide open by the grace of God, he had a terribly profound need of grace and forgiveness himself, but he could not reconcile the two in his own heart. The bondage of the prison in which the law had held him for so many decades led to his death in the inky Seine that chilly night.

As we recall our tendency to swing the pendulum from law to grace, we have to remember that the two don't function apart from one another. Without the law inspiring and illustrating our need for a Savior, we don't understand how sinful and wretched we are, and we certainly cannot see how in need we are of grace. Without grace, we drown in the guilt and shame of our sin, or we run ourselves to death on that miserable treadmill that is all our misappropriated attempts to keep the law.

Our tendency to pendulum swing from law to grace, and from the world's promises to religion's promises could take us down, as it has for so many hopeless people like us throughout history. What we must acknowledge and understand and remind ourselves here, however, is that there is a third, beautiful pendulum-halting middle position, where Jesus Christ and the cross stand firmly. It is here where we may cascade to a positive, surrendered position: In the that humble station of resting where Christ resides, we begin to understand how the grace of God really is greater than all our sin, and how Jesus fulfilled the law.

Should we obey the law? Why, yes, because it

often acts as a guardrail and a buffer to our suffering and destruction. Should we put our hope there? Never, because the law was never meant to fulfill and restore us to God. The law may feel safe for the time being, but our true safety and hope is in the arms of Jesus, who came to fulfill the law and stands with our great God in heaven, our true and only hope of safety.

(1) Hugo, Victor. tr. Lee Fahnestock & Norman MacAfee, *Les Misérables*, Signet Classics, New York: 1987

(2) Ibid.

Questions to Ask Yourself

1. Do you identify with Inspector Javert—nurturing a self-satisfaction that springs from virtuous behavior?

2. Finding the "sweet spot" where law and grace coincide can be a lifelong pursuit for many believers. What are the barriers in your own heart to allowing grace to have the upper hand in the law/grace equation?

3. Do you find it difficult to show grace to yourself? Why do you think you struggle with that?

4. Take the time to think through some of the foundational reasons you might be struggling with the concept that grace triumphs over law-keeping. Some factors may stem from your childhood, how your parents did or did not show grace, how they communicated their acceptance of and love for you, churches you've been a part of, employment situations, relationships, etc.

Chapter 4 –
Evangelizing a
Lifestyle

The University of California at Berkeley sits on an inspiring plot of land. Educating nearly 42,000 students, UC Berkeley turns out some of the world's most influential scholars in tech, medicine, academia, and the arts.

But UC Berkeley also has a colorful history: from 1960's hippie-movement sit-ins and marijuana smoke-ins to left-wing political rallies to a lively, wholesome rivalry between its football team and Stanford University's.

It was in this setting that a young woman found God. He shows up in what we think are the most unlikely of places, doesn't he? She had been marching as a militant feminist, angry at men, angry at God, angry at herself. Into that bitterness and bite, God gently showed her love—genuine love—

and drew her to his truth and healing. She met Jesus on that liberal, colorful campus.

Almost from the moment her soul was saved from death, she made changes in the way she was living from day to day. There were external choices that followed the transformation of her soul: She found herself being kinder to her fellow students simply because she was developing a heart of compassion; she understood their need and wanted them to have what she had found. That's as it should be! Who of us is transformed by the love of God and doesn't then want to turn and tell the people we love about what he's done for us?

She was passionate, even zealous, and all too soon her enthusiasm was met with disdain and rejection. No one wanted what she had found, it seemed. She was hurt, but not deterred. She kept learning to follow Jesus.

When she found a Bible study on campus, she was overjoyed that there were others like her, but most of them had been following Christ for a long time. They knew so much! They'd memorized Bible verses as kids in AWANA and church camps and they had a lingo that was completely new to her. They said things like, "This morning in my quiet time . . .", and, "We just prayed a hedge of protection around them." She was, admittedly, confused, but at the same time, learning the lingo made her feel like she was "getting it". Like somehow, she was becoming a better Christian and God would be pleased.

She observed how they dressed, how they related to one another, how they approached other believers, and how they did or did not engage with unbelievers. This, she felt, was what it meant to be a Christian. She understood that the gospel was a free gift of grace; it had gotten her "in". Now she was being shown what to do.

Sound familiar? The details of her story may vary from yours, but the move toward adopting certain behaviors within Christianity and assigning an ethereal level of spirituality to them is familiar to every follower of Christ. Before we realize it, we find it difficult to extricate what it means to follow Jesus—to be a disciple—from how a particular Christian subculture behaves around one another. And it isn't just cults and the uber conservative who do this.

For the sake of clarification, I'm not describing authentic discipleship. Yes, of course we want to be more like Christ, but that's a genuine work of sanctification, and Scripture makes it clear that sanctification is led and fulfilled by the Holy Spirit (1). Try as we might, we cannot muster up anything that creates true change in our hearts and habits apart from Christ.

Think about it: The modern church lingo and cultural practices where I am in the world (North America) aren't the same as those practiced by believers in Africa or South America or Asia or the Philippines. Heck. I'm from California, and our flip flop/t-shirt/hang loose style isn't practiced in a lot of churches in the other 49 United States. In fact, all of our modern and cultural practices aren't how the church behaved at any other time in history, either.

Yet, so many of us find ourselves evangelizing a lifestyle instead of a savior.

Our new believer finding community at Cal Berkeley soon began to date a fellow student in the group, and together they embraced the confines of a particular Christian religious group. She drastically changed her clothing choices, equating her extreme modesty with pleasing God.

Don't overthink what I'm telling you about this sweet woman; modesty is a way in which we can love and honor others well and not find our identity or self-worth in flaunting what we've got. But extreme modesty links our clothing and style and dress to how pleased we think God is with us. One is about a heart bent on loving people as Christ loved the church and the other is about assigning a behavior to a measurement of how well we keep the rules.

By the time I met her, she was married with a few small children. Her dress hem skirted the floor, her hair was uncut, she was as submissive to her husband as the proverbial doormat, and she was making sure everyone else kept the rules, too.

We had lunch one summer Sunday after church in their home, and it was made very clear that none of the actual cooking had been done on that day, so that the Sabbath would not be tarnished by their work. From the opening conversation about when and how they prepared the meal to when and how they homeschool their children to when and how they worshipped (and with whom and under which teachers and at what time and without which instruments), we were being schooled in the lifestyle they had chosen to live.

At what point do we begin to proselytize others to our choices? My assumption here is that most of us don't at first set out to do this. Initially, we are bowled over by the simple gospel, and we are excited about the relief and peace and joy that comes rushing in as new believers. We become fervent, sometimes even overly annoying, as we share our newfound faith with our friends and family.

But then we begin to learn how to behave. Many of us think, rather guilelessly, "Yeah, yeah, I get the gospel. Now tell me what to do." We begin to scorn the gospel—the pure good news of Jesus Christ's death, burial, and resurrection on our behalf and God's forgiveness of our sins—as the "milk".

We erroneously believe that what Paul is saying to the church at Corinth when he tells them, "But I, brothers, could not address you as spiritual people, but as people of the flesh, as infants in Christ. I fed you with milk, not solid food, for you were not ready for it. And even now you are not yet ready, for you are still of the flesh. For while there is jealousy and strife among you, are you not of the flesh and behaving only in a human way? "(2), is that those simple truths are less important than the solid food of more advanced teaching.

What Paul is actually addressing is the contention and infighting that was occurring in the church at Corinth over who listened to whom and who followed which teachers. This was basic immature human behavior (picture a classroom of 2nd graders arguing dramatically, "Oh yeah? Well I follow Paul!") and Paul is emphasizing that these folks desperately needed a good solid reminder of Whose they were and what Christ had done for them. They needed the gospel. They needed, as he again confirms in 1 Peter, the simple gospel milk to nourish them.

"Like newborn infants, long for the pure spiritual milk, that by it you may grow up into salvation—if indeed you have tasted that the Lord is good." (3)

I love the part about growing up into salvation. Think of it like this:

When a toddler is learning to obey, we don't give them a chart or a list to follow. There is no long and convoluted speech in which we attempt to communicate, "In order to be a good toddler, you must wear these clothes and do exactly what I tell you to do." Can you imagine handing a 2-year-old a list like this?

1. Play with wooden toys. No plastics allowed.
2. Vegetables and fruit only. No candy allowed.

3. Say please and thank you at all times.
4. Make your bed every day.
5. Go to church.

It's ridiculous, isn't it? How does a small child actually learn our values and "house rules"? By abiding with us in our homes, living life together, and walking alongside. If we value a certain toy over another or have deemed some as inappropriate for our home, we eventually communicate that to our growing children with a back story of our values, or at least a simple explanation as to why we do or do not have those things in our home. And the child learns to trust our parental voices.

A child grows up immersed in the "milk" of who we are and what we value. If it's the gospel, then the knowledge that they are loved by God because of what Jesus did for them permeates every corner of the home. From that milk grows a healthy and nourished soul, ready to learn more about Biblical faith, but thoroughly rooted and satiated in the firm foundation of God's love for them.

Pastor and author Timothy Keller states it so beautifully when he claims, "We never "get beyond the gospel" in our Christian life to something more "advanced." The gospel is not the first "step" in a "stairway" of truths, rather, it is more like the "hub" in a "wheel" of truth. The gospel is not just the A-B-C's but the A-Z of Christianity. The gospel is not just the minimum required doctrine necessary to enter the kingdom, but the way we make progress in the kingdom." (4)

Whenever, however, we must never move our thinking beyond the totality of what Jesus did for us at Calvary. From that complete and nourishing milk of our faith and doctrine grows our deepening understanding of it all, and that takes time spent in the presence of God. That's the hard part: time spent with God. It's just easier to follow a list, wear the "right" clothes, say the "right" things, go to the "right" church, make all the "right" choices. Spending time with God, practicing what it means to be in his presence, allowing him to change us from the inside out, learning his voice and knowing his attributes—this is the center of our faith and orthopraxy.

> Whenever, however, we must never move our thinking beyond the totality of what Jesus did for us at Calvary.

The gospel, spending time with God, learning to live in the light of his love for us—that is the A-Z of Christianity.

As you're leaving legalism, do you see where you may have been evangelizing a lifestyle rather than the gospel of Jesus Christ? For most of us, it's time to get back to the nourishing milk of truth.

(1) 1 Thessalonians 5:23, John 17:17, Galatians 2:20, 2 Thessalonians 2:13, and many more

(2) 1 Corinthians 3:1-3

(3) 1 Peter 2:2

(4) Keller, Timothy, *Center Church*, Zondervan, 2012

Questions to Ask Yourself

1. Can you look back and see how you may have been evangelized to a particular lifestyle? What did that look like?

2. Do you see where you may have been evangelizing a lifestyle?

3. How long has it been since you really spent time immersed in the solid spiritual milk of the simple gospel?

4. What might you do to remind yourself of what God has done for you through Jesus Christ?

Chapter 5 – Your Identity in Christ

I have a beautiful young friend from Brazil. Dani moved to the United States after marrying her husband, an American, whom she met while he was working in South America with a missions organization. Moving a continent away wasn't easy for Dani, even though she was happy to do so because she loves her husband and was excited to grow her architecture and design firm in a new country.

One day just a year or two after she had moved to California, Dani and I met for a sushi lunch. Her English was slightly halted, though not a barrier to our conversation, but she began to tell me her frustrations with trying to make a community here for herself.

"In Brazil, everyone knows they can just drop in to see friends at anytime. It's so strange that in America, people don't do that. I don't really know if I'm ever bothering someone if I ring their doorbell and they weren't expecting me."

She also talked about the need to improve her English because she felt she was missing cues and not always understanding the intent of a conversation.

In some of the most essential areas of our lives and relationships (how and when we communicate), Dani felt she had lost her identity.

About the same time I met Dani, I met Pips. Like Dani, Pips had moved to the United States after marrying her husband, but she was leaving a whole life in South Africa behind.

Pips told me that one of the most difficult things about making a life here is that she isn't just Pips anymore. She's "the South African girl", or, "You know, Pips. She's from South Africa." She says it's strange to be identified like that because growing up in South Africa, she was described and known by who she is, what her personality is like, whose child or sister she is. Suddenly, she's been assigned a whole new identity as Pips-the-South-African.

Neither Dani nor Pips expected a crisis of identity when they chose to move their lives across the world. Neither likely even gave their identity a thought prior to making their life-changing moves, and like them, we very often don't think about our own identities, either.

I grew up in the American evangelical church, surrounded by solid preachers both in the churches where I was involved and on the radio. My parents believed in a "Berean"-type approach to Biblical teaching: Hear what the preacher is saying and then take it back to Scripture to see if it is sound. I'm certain that in all of those years of hearing sermons, somewhere along the line someone said, "Your identity is in Jesus."

It's one of those things that I knew, but I didn't know.

If you don't know (or if you've forgotten), your identity is in Christ, too:

"But whoever is joined to the Lord becomes one spirit with him." 1 Corinthians 6:17

"Now you are the body of Christ and individually members of it." 1 Corinthians 12:27

"But you are a chosen race, a royal priesthood, a holy nation, a people for his own possession, that you may proclaim the excellencies of him who called you out of darkness into his marvelous light." 1 Peter 2:9

And that's barely scratching the surface. Keep going! Be a Berean and look up all of the verses that tell us our identity is in the one who made us and the whole universe, loved us even when we were rotten sinners, loves us still as rotten sinners, and all because of what Jesus Christ did on the cross.

What that means, in the heady realm of theology, is that when God looks at us, he sees Jesus. That's mind-blowing, isn't it? I mean, that should completely rock our world. He doesn't see me—the failure, the weak, the seemingly insignificant—he sees perfect Jesus.

So when the voices of legalism and the leaders in your past church community acted as the Holy Spirit in your life and told you how you should behave and what you should do and how you should dress, parent, be married, be single, work, worship, and rest, you can now override all of that spiritual abuse by reminding yourself daily of the simple truth that your identity is solidly, unshakably in Jesus. You are literally hidden in Christ.

When God looks at you, he sees Jesus. Those aren't my words. They are his:

"If then you have been raised with Christ, seek the things that are above, where Christ is, seated at the right hand of God. Set your minds on things that are above, not on things that are on earth. For you have died, and your life is hidden with Christ in God. When Christ who is your life appears, then you also will appear with him in glory." (1)

And here's the thing we must cement into our thinking: All of that covering and commitment to us by Christ is the result of what he has done, not of what we have done. Rigid communities want to place standards and rules and restrictions and behaviors that tell us that if we live up to them, we will be loved by God. But it's the exact reverse.

The truth is, God sent a rescuer because we are at our worst.

The truth is, God loves us even when we are at our worst.

The truth is, God will set about doing the work of sanctification in our lives when we are at our worst.

This is the opposite of what we legalists think. In our legalism, we embrace a formula that adds our works to his pleasure. But God's pleasure precedes our efforts. God's not mad at us. He's certainly not disappointed in us. He loves us relentlessly.

> Rigid communities want to place standards and rules and restrictions and behaviors that tell us that if we live up to them, we will be loved by God. But it's the exact reverse.

In the 2017 film *The Heart of Man*, the gentle and loving father whose character symbolizes God crafts a gorgeous violin for his son, painstakingly carving the rich wood and threading the strings exactly where they need to be. He then patiently teaches him to play the instrument with passion and skill. Their relationship as father and son is deep and close, and their affection for one another is obvious. They work together, they play music together, they live life in cadence with one another.

As the story develops, we see the son mature into a young man and bit by bit, uncover a longing for what lies beyond the peaceful land where he dwells with his father and their loving community. He is lured by the unknown, by his imagination, by what might lie across the sea on the island just beyond the scruffy cliff and choppy water.

The Heart of Man is a film I think every believer needs to see, and so with that in mind, I'm not going to spoil it for you in case you haven't seen it yet. But just as the prodigal son left home in search of something he was so sure was better than what his father had for him at home, the young man in the movie leaves on a quest to satiate the lust in his heart for what is over the horizon. And as you might have guessed, it doesn't pan out the way he had hoped.

Eventually, at the end of his rope, beaten, tormented, without hope, the son musters his last ounce of human strength to lift his head and see through the dim light that his father has arrived to rescue the child he loves so profoundly. He is there, carrying his battered son on his back, restoring him to health, returning the violin to his hands, playing his song of deliverance and redemption. He never stopped loving or pursuing his son, not even when his son had abandoned him. Not even when his son was at his rotten worst.

It's the most beautiful and accurate picture of the God who saves that I have ever seen. When we showed *The Heart of Man* to our children, even our 11-year-old son wept.

And that God—relentlessly pursuing, readily loving, steadfastly chasing us—that is the God with whom our identity rests into eternity. We cannot make him mad enough to cut us off. Our salvation is about what he has done, not what we must do.

If we can remember that, we will have understood the gospel. If we can replace all of the yuck we weathered in churches and communities that told us we had to measure up to some arbitrary standard with the truth that our identity is as hidden in Christ, we can begin to heal.

> If we can replace all of the yuck we weathered in churches and communities that told us we had to measure up to some arbitrary standard with the truth that our identity is as hidden in Christ, we can begin to heal.

Even if the church we were in held to simple Biblical standards—even then—we must remember that the markers of our faith, the behaviors that the Bible tells us accompany someone who loves and follows Christ, the Biblical standards for Christian living, are not what cement our salvation. They are not our identity.

But God is. Jesus Christ is. The Holy Spirit is. It is their work, their mercy, their grace, their compassion, and their character that make us who we are, and in the midst of our worst, *they love us anyway.* It's totally backwards from how we humans operate. We're pretty driven to love people based on their behavior. Isn't it a good thing we're not God?

When we see the "therefores" in Scripture, we have to remember that those passages begin with "therefore" because they are preceded by the foundation of God's love for us. The "therefore" of Ephesians chapter four is built on three previous chapters where Paul explains the gospel—the milk—the nourishing truth of God's deep love, Christ's sacrifice on our behalf, and our security in him. It is his work that compels us to obey him. He is pleased with us because of his work. He loves us because of his work. It is this knowledge, reiterated throughout long passages in the gospels to remind us, that serves to touch us deeply and drives us to a passionate desire to love God and love others.

I know that believing we are loved in spite of our behavior or choices or humanity is a long leap for many of us. We feel so unloved and we cannot fathom that we are loved in a way that requires nothing from us. But this is the gospel. This is Jesus Christ himself. And you know what? He loves us so much that he doesn't leave us as we are. He begins to work in our hearts and lives to change us from the inside out. All of that behavior and Christian living and markers of our faith are graciously and lovingly wrought by him, for his glory and our good.

Knowing how loved we are by God and knowing that our identity is in him is truly the first step to freedom from religion and the legalism that crushes.

"I have been crucified with Christ; and it is no longer I who live, but Christ lives in me; and the life which I now live in the flesh I live by faith in the Son of God, who loved me and gave Himself up for me." Galatians 2:20

(1) Colossians 3:1-4

Extra reading if you're struggling to believe the depth of God's love for you:

Because He Loves Me, Elyse Fitzpatrick, Crossway, 2010

The Gift of Being Yourself: The Sacred Call to Self-Discovery, David G. Benner, IVP Books, 2015

The Saving Life of Christ, Major Ian Thomas, Zondervan, 1989

Questions to Ask Yourself

1. Typically we humans find our identity in our careers, homes, marriages, children, and relationships. It can be humiliating and painful when we realize that we have been finding our identity in anything other than Christ. In what things have you been finding your identity?

2. The most important foundational concept for living free in Christ is understanding God's love for us and then living as loved. Is it difficult for you to believe that you are loved by God, no matter what? Why do you think you struggle to believe that?

3. List three practical, tangible ways you can daily remind yourself that you are loved by God.

Chapter 6 – Unfurling Your Grip

We have a 10-year-old boy with special needs. On the outside, Mighty Joe looks "normal". He looks just like any other 10-year-old boy: a little dirty most of the time, t-shirts and flip flops preferred, hair sticking up unless someone has gotten to it before we head out the door. But inside of his brain and neurological system, something else entirely is going on. The six holes left by encephalitis when the virus attacked his body as a baby cause all kinds of daily havoc. He melts down when life is too hard, which is every day. He has seizures that last an unreasonable amount of time. He talks too loudly and he eats too fast and he runs when he should be walking. He's really only about 5 years old emotionally and developmentally.

We love to take Joe and our other kids to Disneyland, but Disneyland with Joe is a "next level" event. He doesn't really do crowds and chaos and noise and running from ride to ride and, well, Disneyland, but he does agree that it is the happiest place on earth. As with most 5-year-olds, we can't tell him we're planning to go there or he'll obsess and drive us crazy until our feet actually get out of the car to hit the Disneyland parking lot.

For Joe and many kids, Disneyland is the stuff of dreams.

And yet, as we walk to each next ride, Joe must talk about it. He needs to know what exactly the ride is all about, if it goes real high, how long we'll wait in line, what we will do on the ride, if it's scary, if it's winding, if we'll get wet. He must talk about the characters if it happens to be a ride built around Winnie-the-Pooh or Indiana Jones, and he must talk himself into the entire experience before we hit the back of the queue.

Even on the most innocuous and innocent of rides (the carousel, for instance), Joe works himself into a bundle of agitation and anxiety.

I have a picture on my phone of Joe's small hand gripped tightly around my wrist. I took that picture the last time we were in Disneyland, because it was such a good reminder of how Joe lives life: full of excitement and energy and simultaneously scared to death. He seizes my arm like that any time he can't cope with what is being thrown at him.

I think that's how a lot of us live our lives, too. On the one hand, we are excited about what's ahead. We plan big job moves and look forward with anticipation to the big life decisions, but we hold on with all our strength, terrified of the changes ahead and walking into what is the unknown.

We grip, we grasp, we squeeze, we hold on as tightly as we can to the familiar.

We grip even when we know we need to leave a tough or toxic situation. We grasp at what is known to us, even if it's been abusive to us. We squeeze, hoping that by doing so, the circumstances might change in our favor. We hold on as tightly as we can, because the known is often less scary than the unknown, even if the unknown will mean we can walk out unshackled and live free.

I met Marie at the beginning of my senior year of high school, in our required economics class. She was one of the cool girls, always included at the parties for popular people and the big high school stuff like decorating the gym for homecoming or sitting amongst all the big-men-and-women-on-campus at the football games. I wasn't one of them. I was a musical theater geek.

I don't suspect Marie expected we'd become friends that year. I certainly didn't assume so, and was pretty happily fixed in my world of actors and performers and the local dinner theater. I left school in the afternoon, took a dance class or music lesson, made sure my homework was done, and hung out at the theater for rehearsal or performances until 11pm most nights. My world was decidedly not Marie's world.

She sat in front of me. At the beginning of the school year, it was an agreeable seating chart because we didn't really talk to each other. We weren't orbiting the same high school planet with the same high school people. But by mid-December, our senior economics teacher Mr. Briggs was probably pretty sorry he'd sat Marie and I next to each other.

We talked. A lot (and rarely on the subject of economics). By the time our June graduation came around, we were solid friends, deeply involved in each other's lives and swearing our allegiance into the college years ahead of us. Marie went off to the beaches of UC Santa Barbara and I was six hours away at California's oldest university just off the San Joaquin Delta.

One brisk late October evening Marie called me. I leaned my back against the door of my dorm room and spoke quietly to her as I sat in the hallway and tried not to disturb the other girls on my floor. The phone cord stretched under the door from my bedside; it was the fall of 1988 and our phones were still tethered to the wall.

"I met an amazing guy here!" Marie gushed. "I mean, we slept together the first night. I never thought I'd do that, but the sex was magical." My little naive heart raised in conservative evangelicalism almost stopped. Marie wasn't a

Christian, so I didn't really expect her to make a commitment to any one guy until she married someone, but still—first date? Really?

I didn't know how to respond, so I kept listening. "Kendra, I've been smoking shrooms with my friends here. I can't even tell you how incredible and transformative it is. The hallucinations are life-altering. Seriously. When we get together over Christmas break, you've got to do this with me. It will change your life."

Marie had always been a fervent seeker of spiritual things. Raised in a liberal Jewish home, she understood the power of faith and we talked often of our differing viewpoints. She came to church with me, sat in the wooden pews under the light streaming through the centuries-old stained glass, and remarked on the formality of my Presbyterian minister as he preached fervently from the wooden pulpit high above the sanctuary. I visited her formidable synagogue and sincerely enjoyed the personable nature of her rabbi as he sauntered between the rows of chairs and engaged his congregation from his heart.

In all of our discussions, I tried to make her understand why the gospel is special and why Jesus fulfilled all that her Jewish faith was longing for, but in the end, she told me, "That's right for you. I'm glad you have Jesus. But it isn't what I'm looking for."

My heart ached for my friend. I knew she was empty and searching and needing to fill the infinite abyss in her soul that longed desperately for truth. At just 18 years old, I felt helpless to stop her heading down the track that took her on a journey of following that eccentric man she met her freshman year of college.

Turns out, he was more dangerous than any of us would initially understand. He whisked Marie away to Albuquerque, New Mexico where he begin to form a cult, a small band of seekers like Marie who believed he could offer the answers to the questions they were asking about meaning and the universe. I didn't see Marie for 25 years.

During those several decades, Marie's family did everything they could to try and get her out. She had a child, they knew, because they would travel to Albuquerque periodically to try to convince her to leave the cult and the oppressive living situation she was in. From their parked car, secretly observing the home where the cult members lived together, they watched a small child who looked like Marie playing on the lawn — a precious tiny blonde girl — and they believed she was the child of Marie and the cult leader.

In all of that time of waiting and watching, I prayed with a gnawing ache in my gut for Marie. A miniature photograph of us together in high school placed in a gold heart-shaped frame lived on my desk reminding me each time I glanced up at it to pray for her freedom.

One evening just a few years ago as I was mindlessly scrolling my Facebook feed, a picture popped up unexpectedly. Another old friend from high school was visiting Albuquerque and posted a photo of her with Marie, whom I instantly recognized. She was my same beautiful high school friend, 25 years older.

"Look who I found!", our mutual friend wrote. I began to weep, right there, staring with wonder and awe at my laptop screen. I yelled to my family, "You guys! Come look at this! I can't believe it!" Immediately I messaged the other friend to inquire about Marie. Was she reachable?

She reluctantly was, but it wasn't until Marie herself took a brave leap into social media and we found each other once again there on Facebook that we could talk to each other, catching up, trying to make up for lost time, 25 years later.

Had Marie found freedom from the cult? Yes, but like Joe's nervous grip around my wrist as we ride every Disneyland attraction, she couldn't remove her own furled grip from the familiarity of the cult community she'd been known by for so many years. Year after year, yearning for peace, Marie hoped and longed for something better but she couldn't move herself in the direction of freedom. It was too hard. Too scary. Too unknown and unfamiliar. The world had changed a lot in 25 years.

What she had lost while in bondage to her fear of leaving the familiarity of the cult were the basic desires of many of our human hearts. She was long-estranged from her two children, who had at one point been rescued by her family and given new lives in stability and their family community. She had abandoned the college degree she was once aspiring to earn. She had, essentially, lost two decades of a life that felt stolen from her as she had placed her hope in the promises of a cult leader who stepped in to take the place of the authentic savior, Jesus Christ.

"I regret so many things", she told me. "But I can't get back what I've lost. I'm free now, and that's what I'm having to remind myself every time my mind is tempted to sink into all of the 'what-if's'."

Marie is not a believer in Jesus. She's still searching, and I realize that's not the tidy ending we Christians want to read about, but it's the truth. I'm still praying and hoping and dreaming for Marie. I'm still talking to her about my Jesus.

From our fear and anxiety about leaving the known for the unknown to mourning the loss of all we missed while deeply entrenched in our legalistic communities, unfurling our grip can be the most excruciatingly difficult thing any of us has had to face, ever. And while we're painstakingly extricating ourselves from the bondage and abuse that kept us there, we can feel very much alone in our journey.

Back in chapter one, I promised that we would talk about what it means to separate our former legalism from the actual act of following Jesus without the wild, sweeping swing of the proverbial pendulum. The thing is, so many of us tend to

KENDRA FLETCHER | 75

swing that pendulum from one end to the other because we're just not sure what it means to unfurl our grip from all that we have known. We flounder and flail, grasping to find stability, trying to define what it means to actually follow Jesus without the trappings of the life we knew before. Without the rules and the rulers who made the rules.

And the answer is as difficult as anything we've covered so far. The answer feels like free-falling. The answer feels as if the foundation has been ripped out from underneath us entirely. The answer feels like we're just throwing open the airplane cabin door and flinging ourselves out into the atmosphere without a guide, a parachute, or a soft landing. The answer is found purely in our relationship with God.

> The answer is found purely in our relationship with God.

That's it.

No, really.

The answer is to abide with Christ. To walk with him. To follow. To keep our eyes fixed on him and no one else. No one else.

No one else.

"What else does this craving, and this helplessness, proclaim but that there was once in man a true happiness, of which all that now remains is the empty print and trace? This he tries in vain to fill with everything around him, seeking in things that are not there the help he cannot find in those that are, though none can help, since this infinite abyss can be filled only with an infinite and immutable object; in other words by God himself." -Blaise Pascal

That's it exactly, and it didn't take the brilliant mind of a gifted mathematician like Blaise Pascal to discover the secret of unfurling our grip and halting the wild pendulum swings and shifting our hope back to Jesus. Jesus himself told us the secret when he said, "If you abide in me, and my words abide in you, ask whatever you wish, and it will be done for you." (1)

He also said, "Abide in me, and I in you. As the branch cannot bear fruit by itself, unless it abides in the vine, neither can you, unless you abide in me." (2)

Abide.

Wouldn't it have been easier if I had titled this chapter "How to Unfurl Your Grip in 12 Easy Steps" and then given you the 12 steps to follow to becoming free in Christ? I actually sighed as I wrote that. An audible sigh, right here at the little outdoor table at Starbucks where I'm writing this morning, because that's really what we law-lovers want. We want to be told what the standard is and then we want to try to meet it in our own strength and pride.

Don't forget: Jesus is the standard. Jesus met the standard for you. It's already met. You've already met it because of him.

So how does one learn to abide in Christ? It

might be easier to wrap our minds around this whole idea of abiding if I put it into our modern vernacular: Hang out with Jesus. Pray. Talk to him. Listen for him. Be quiet. Be still. Walk away for awhile and do the dishes

> Don't forget: Jesus is the standard.

or change the oil. Come back and hang out alone with him. Rest.

Just hanging out with God and resting can seem like a practical impossibility for most of us. If I haven't already mentioned it, I have 8 children. There is rarely a time in our home that is quiet, and where my time belongs only to me. Even now with adult children already moved out, my phone lights up with texts and phone calls from them and/or their spouses on a regular basis, and I'm usually having a conversation with someone well past midnight.

During the day there are school and work and community commitments. Sports and music and side hustles and caring for those in need. Paperwork, holiday prep, reading, research, and home care. Someone has to wash the car and the dog. You might not have a lot of kids, but you have a full plate, too.

There are plenty of books and websites out there to help us learn how to slow down and how to know what to make a daily priority, so I won't go into the practical side of all of that. What I will do is remind us that there are only so many hours in each day, and it is up to us to make a plan to tackle only what God has required of us. For those of us with a strong grip and a drive to do more and try harder, stopping and resting so that we can hear God amongst the clamor seems absolutely impossible.

But I would suggest that learning to recognize God (where he is around us, how he's proven his faithfulness, what he communicates in scripture, what it means to know his peace) is the number one most essential line item of the believer's day. However, I won't suggest that there is only one way to go about it. We recovering legalists have heard plenty of opinions about what time with God "should" look like. The goal of prioritizing "hanging out with God" is singular and very, very simple: When we take the time to slow down all of our doing and trying, we learn to hear God, see God, and be loved by him.

Want to know something wild? When I finally unfurled my grip, walked away from the leaders and the community that were telling me to try harder and do more, and *stopped trying altogether*, I grew more spiritually in those first five years of learning what it means to abide in Christ than I had during the entire 40 years of living a western evangelical Christian lifestyle that took me straight into legalism and all my puny attempts to save myself and make God love me more.

Abiding is simply where the miracle of Christ's work changes us. Try saying this out loud to yourself: It's all Christ's work.

Grace requires nothing of you.

If you absolutely must have something to do because your head won't rest until you feel you're

> Learning to recognize God is the number one most essential line item of the believer's day.

accomplishing something tangible and measurable, read what the gospels and the epistles tell us about abiding in Christ:

John 3:6-9
John 8:31
John 14:17
John 15:4-9
Romans 8:1
2 Corinthians 5:17
Ephesians 3:17-19
Colossians 2:6
1 John 2:24
1 John 2:27
1 John 2:28
1 John 3:24
1 John 4:13
2 John 1:9
Revelation 3:20

A few other practical tools to help you see and know God, to "hang out with him", might be:

Buy a journaling Bible and write notes in the sidebar about each of the passages and verses above. If you're not sure what to write, write the simple gospel: God loves me, Christ died for me, I am free.

Grab a stack of index cards and give yourself the time to write out each of God's truths about abiding in him.

Record the gospel (God loves me, Christ died for me, I am free.) on your phone and play it back to yourself while you drive.

As we learn to lay down all of our former rules and abide in Christ instead, it's a solid idea to remind ourselves repeatedly of the gospel and of God's endless, unprecedented, unearned love for each of us, individually. Learn to rest there. If that seems excruciatingly, ridiculously impossible—if you're squirming at the thought—hang in for another chapter with me. Let's talk about how we can learn to love God again.

(1) John 15:7
(2) John 15:4

Questions to Ask Yourself

1. It might be a long and painful exercise, but it would be worth the time to list all of the extra-biblical rules (both spoken and unspoken) of your former church and/or community. For example, if you were required to be at every worship service offered during the week, or if it was simply frowned upon that you didn't attend each time, write that down.

2. As you think about your life, where did the pressure to follow the rules of the church initially come from?

3. For you, what is the most difficult thing about laying down all of the "have-to's" and "musts" of religion and learning to simply abide in Christ ("Hang out with God") instead?

4. Is there one behavior or rule in particular in your life that will be the most difficult to let go of for the sake of following Jesus alone?

Chapter 7 –
Resting in What
He Has Done
(Loving God)

Royal Robbins was a remarkable man. If you're into rock climbing, you can skip my intro about him, because you undoubtedly know who he was. He's a legend in the world of climbers.

But for the rest of us, here's what you need to know: Royal Robbins was the first person to scale the faces of the monstrous rock formations of Yosemite National Park, such as El Capitan and Half Dome. That second one is the instantly recognizable half-dome so famously photographed by Ansel Adams and a million park visitors since.

What Royal and his climbing buddies did was groundbreaking because they felt strongly about preserving the rocks they ascended, and so they even made their historic climbs without the use of bolts driven into the rocks that would serve as handholds.

Living as close to the Yosemite Valley as we do (it's a day trip we make often), we're always made aware by the local news outlets when a climber falls to his or her death. I don't get used to the reports; I gasp in disbelief and sorrow for them and their loved ones because it seems to me such a shocking way to die, plunging to your death from so many thousands of feet above the ground. Any climber willing to make those ascents knows the dangers and possibilities before they set out to conquer the climb.

Royal was a good acquaintance of our family. He once ran into my husband and our four oldest kids on a nearby trail at Pinecrest Lake and made a detour from his own plans just to teach my kids to climb. He had a kind heart and a generous spirit.

One evening Royal told us a story that occurred on a jutted ridge on the top of Half Dome. If you do a photo search for that ridge, you'll find pictures of it, usually with someone sitting with their legs dangling over the edge, hanging more than 4,737 feet above the valley floor.

Royal made the 400-foot ascent up the backside of Half Dome by way of cables one sunny summer day, and there amongst the climbers enjoying the unparalleled views of Yosemite Valley, a small boy in a red baseball cap ventured out to that precipitous ledge and began to teeter. His father turned to see the boy so close to a fatal fall, and rushed over, scooped him up, and carried him back to safety. From that moment on, for the rest of the time they were on the top of Half Dome, the little boy clung to his father. He never left his side.

Royal told us that witnessing the father saving his son was an illustration to him of the relationship a parent should have with their child—of trust and faith and security and loyalty.

In the child's understanding of what he was saved from and his newfound love and gratitude for what his father had done for him, the child desired nothing more than to stay glued to the father, to listen to his voice, and to obey him all the way back down the descent of Half Dome.

How like God the father in Royal's story is. And how much more we see our God protecting, loving, and stepping in to save us. If we can't see it in the moment, we can see his hand in history. Someday that little boy may doubt his father's love or wonder where he's been, but he'll be able to remember back to the day on Half Dome when his father saved his life and know that the character of his father was to love, protect, and carry his son.

It can be difficult to emerge from years of spiritual abuse at the hands of people who should have loved us like Christ. It can be impossible to look back and see where God was at work in our lives then and even more confusing to see where He might be at work in our lives right now. The truthful answer for many of us to the question, "Where do you see God at work in your life?", is often, "I don't."

So what do we do? We rest (abide) in His finished work. We begin to, as that little boy did, live as loved children of the living God. The little boy knew by the swift action of his father that he was valued and loved by him, and he felt safe and secure in his identity as the loved-boy-of-his-father. That's the whole point of God. He loves us. He loves us. Say it to yourself, out loud: He loves me.

Whisper it. Write it on your mirror, speak it into your voice recorder on your phone and play it back. However you need to hear it, however often you need to be reminded, tell yourself this rock-solid truth: God loves me.

I know I keep repeating this point, but it bears daily repeating in each of our lives: The God we put our hope in proclaimed as he hung on the cross carrying the wicked burden of all of our sin, "It is finished." He bore our weight and all the risk when he stepped onto the precipitous ledge

> He kept the law so that we don't have to.

to save us from plunging to our deaths. He kept the law so that we don't have to.

Have you ever heard the hymn, "How Deep the Father's Love For Us"? (1) It's a tender and profoundly satisfying song that reminds us of God's deep love for us, and I'm always pleased to hear it pop up wherever I might be worshiping on a Sunday morning.

Well into the fourth stanza, the line, "It was our

sin that held him there" has always driven a nail into my guilty conscience, and that's probably as it should be, except that because of what Jesus did for me, I am no longer guilty. He bore the guilt. He bore the shame. I might feel it, but I no longer have to bear it.

God bless the hymn writers because it's no small task to take the truth of Scripture and make something beautiful for us to sing and sear into our worshiping hearts. But in this case, I can't agree with that line. Jesus gives an accurate account of the reason he stayed on the cross that day:

"For this reason the Father loves me, because I lay down my life that I may take it up again. No one takes it from me, but I lay it down of my own accord. I have authority to lay it down, and I have authority to take it up again. This charge I have received from my Father." (2)

It wasn't my sin that held him there; it was his love. His love for the father, his love for the world, his love for me.

When we deeply and truly believe this, we can change our prayer from, "Help me do more and keep the law better so that you'll forgive me and love me", to, "Help me believe you more." Help me love you more.

When we take God at his word and believe how loved we are by him, everything else in our lives is transformed correspondingly.

Like the little boy on the precipitous edge, our response to God's love for us is awe and gratitude, and that compels us to serve Him, follow Him, and love Him. But our service, our following, and our love do not make him love us any more than he already does. Serving, following, and loving are by-products of what Jesus has already accomplished. He said, "It is finished" (remember?) There is nothing we add to that. Nothing.

Learning to live as loved and learning to love God resemble in their essence the whole seemingly celestial concept of abiding in Christ that we touched on in the last chapter.

It is in the moments of relationship and walking with and following that we learn to love and know God better, but there's no one who can really impart to us how to do that, and the frustration of flying blind can be a deal-killer for those of us who are used to checklists and formulas. Just give me the list! Just tell me what I am supposed to do. I'd feel more productive.

When our oldest boys were quite little, they were part of a 9-member cousin band of all boys. I have two brothers, and all three of us produced three boys each before any girls were born. It was all boys, all the time, and we sister-in-law moms often felt in over our heads. Little boys are a lot of things: loud, dirty, energetic, often inappropriate, silly, and obsessed with bodily functions.

I remember being on the phone one evening with my oldest brother's wife, whom I would call often just to pick her brain about the parenting of these miniature male people. Her boys were a couple of years older than mine, and she had already traversed the bumpy path just ahead of me.

"Kendra, God gave me a picture this week", she told me. "It was a vision of me sitting at a long wooden table that was stacked with books two feet high, and as I looked closer I realized that they were all parenting books. Every single one."

I could relate to this. I was a fast and furious inhaler of parenting advice.

"But then God said something so clear to me, something so undeniably for me, that I've had to stop and reassess what I've been doing. He said, 'Laura, close the books.' I think he wants me to tune out all of the advice and wisdom of the so-called parenting experts and just listen to him."

I'll be honest: That didn't sit well with me. In fact, it made me squirm a little. Close the books? Turn away from the human experts and look to Christ instead? What did that even mean?

At the time, I was a 20-something young mom with a whole lot of "how-to's" attached to my Christianity and pitifully few miles logged on the long road just getting to know Jesus. It made me extremely uncomfortable to dump the practical advice and put my hand in Christ's. I'll say it again: I didn't even know what that meant.

Maybe you've been reading this whole book with that response, too. Remember how I introduced the concept of abiding in Christ as a freefall? That might still be bothering you, and that's okay. The thing about the love of God is that its depth and purity is so beyond our comprehension that it can be a lifelong process to get to a place where we understand that he loves us anyway. I'm going to go out on a limb and venture that most of us may never get to the place where we understand even a small fraction of what God's love for us truly means.

He loves us even if we never understand it, even if we never get to that place where we can freefall without feeling as if we're going to throw up. Even then.

> He loves us even if we never understand it…

So really, it's about surrendering to him, too. Surrendering our understanding of who he is. Surrendering our listless attempts at pleasing him. Even surrendering to the work that he is doing in our hearts, in spite of our brokenness and lack of understanding of who he is.

For those of us who love to live according to our lists, the concept of surrendering seems nebulous and intangible. Maybe this is the first step in a walk of faith that doesn't rely on a man-made measuring stick? Ask God to help you lay down your work and striving and attempts to please him. Ask God to help you learn to live as loved.

David G. Benner wrote, "Only God deserves absolute surrender because only God can offer absolutely dependable love." If for no other reason than this, surrender to God because he so dependably loves you.

(1) Stuart Townend, "How Deep the Father's Love For Us", Say the Word, Integrity Music, 2007
(2) John 10:17-18

Questions to Ask Yourself

1. Do you picture God as a loving rescuer?

2. Are you okay with the fact that getting to know God is a long, slow, lifelong, relationship that will stretch into eternity, and we can't know everything about him all at once?

3. Have you asked God to help you live as loved? What do you see as a barrier to believing the scope of his love for you?

Chapter 8
How to Move Forward
(Including How to Apologize to Your Children)

The night we took our two oldest boys to a coffee shop to sit them down and apologize for raising them in such a graceless home and community was dark and hot and felt like a breathless walk into a courtroom where the verdict is left with a hung jury.

They were 17 and 15. They'd spent the bulk of their childhoods trying to meet our constricted standards of behavior, and they'd learned to be great little Pharisees: our "mini-me's". Now that we were out of that airless environment, our kids were learning to breathe on their own. We were all trying to figure out what it meant to be Christians without our former man-created and man-enforced rules and regulations, but the air we were newly breathing was full of the pure oxygen of God's grace.

Only a couple of months had passed since we'd left our legalistic church, and here we found ourselves in a bustling coffee house, hoping to recover and restore our wounded relationships with our sons. As if the teenage years aren't difficult enough to traverse. Their dad led the way:

"Guys, we just want to apologize to you. We earnestly thought we were making the right choices and raising you in a way that honored God. Instead, we became legalistic and rigid and demanding, and that was worse than wrong. It was Godless. It was destructive."

He paused to take a deep breath.

"We see where we had put all of our hope in all the wrong things, and for that, we are sincerely sorry."

There were fresh, sorrowful tears, both for the boys and for us. They initially didn't really say anything as they sat with their hands folded in their laps and processed the words we were respectfully offering to them, and then, quietly—just like that— they forgave us.

For so many reasons, that conversation felt like running into a burning building. We hoped to salvage as much as we could in our relationships with them—anything, really—but we knew that in order to do so, we were probably going to get burned in the process. Their quick forgiveness was not without pain and a long road to healing, but we would never have known what restoration might lie ahead had we not taken the risk that facing the fire required.

Moving forward in our relationships with the people we may have wounded while we were running headlong into religion more often than not means we must "run into the burning building", and likely more than once. It scalds. It blisters. There's wreckage. But nothing can be salvaged unless we courageously run face forward into the flames and lay down our lives for the sake of restoring relationships.

If you do this, I can't promise that everything will be saved. Firefighters run into the burning building in order to rescue anything they can, but sometimes, the building burns to the ground. Sometimes the hurt we've caused is too deep in the life of the other person, and all we can do is own our sin, apologize sincerely, and pray that the Holy Spirit will begin to work in the other person's life. We can't force their forgiveness. We can't always save what has been lost. Sometimes the building spontaneously combusts as we're trying to scrap anything we can.

Our boys were extremely accepting of our repentance that night. Their forgiveness was immediate but the healing has not been. And I'll pause right here to make this point: There is no guarantee that those in need of an apology in your life will be as quick to forgive as our sons initially were. To tell you so would be disingenuous. It's not my intent to give you false hope.

Still, we know that our obedience to God always brings about healing in some form or another, even if the desired outcome of a completely restored relationship is not reached during our life on this earth. We ask for forgiveness as an act of obedience and then we let God do the heavy lifting.

> We ask for forgiveness as an act of obedience and then we let God do the heavy lifting.

For us, the healing has come in small fits and starts, in our children observing us throwing off the constraints of religious adherence, in the choices we make that reflect that we are in this walk of faith for the long haul.

For us, the healing has come by way of marinating ourselves in the grace of God, in granting ourselves the grace we so desperately lack. Who are we to assign more condemnation to ourselves than Jesus Christ himself does? And yet, that's really what so many of us do as we chase rules and lists and behaviors in the place of resting, following, and believing in his work on our behalf.

One of our sons battles serious mental illness, and within that dark and desperate space, we have had to trust God more than ever. He has struggled to see God in his suffering, because his suffering has been personal and terrible. The last five years of his life read like a really bad movie plot, with twists and turns that stem from the mixed up messages moving like a ticker tape through his brain. Learning to love himself has been a long, slow process because in our former church, the messages he received were laced with judgment and an underlying high voltage current of, "You're not measuring up."

For someone battling mental instability and chemical imbalance his entire young life, no amount of good behavior would ever match our former church's made-up standards. And in the hyper-religious system where we were surrounded by the morality gate-keepers, medications and psychiatrists would never be embraced. Everything was labeled a spiritual issue.

I remember when he was about 14 and he came to me with clenched fists and spouted out his anguished words behind frustrated, hot tears:

"I feel like I can never do anything right!"

His frustration was punctuated by defeat; he had lost the religious game within the community that was supposed to be loving him, and he could not see clear to love even himself.

My weary mom-heart shattered as I realized the heavy desperation in his words. "You're right. You can't. We haven't given you the space to succeed at anything."

I hugged that young man tight, sobbing with him, and I knew we had to see a way forward that allowed us to love him in the trickiness of who he is. We have failed at this repeatedly, but if nothing else, he has heard us tell him over and over again, "You are loved". Even though he is now a fully-grown adult man in his mid-20's, we often have conversations that are laced with words of Biblical truth so that his soul can be nourished by the grace and love of Christ.

Just this week I texted him, "God created you. He loves you. He loves you better, truer, more completely, more in spite of your junk than anyone ever will. You are loved because he loves you. You have value because he loves you."

He struggles to believe.

Our religious communities struggle to understand someone like him. We think everyone should be responding and moving forward in their spiritual maturity at the same rate, and we give very little wiggle room for those who struggle differently than we do.

In our church circles and Christian communities, often the word "grace" is whispered like some clandestine dirty scandal and we all start to tense up. I mean, if we show unmerited grace to our neighbor, or even crazier—from the pulpit—suddenly we've opened up Pandora's Box, right?

If we give grace, then people will just do what they want, and we can't have that!

I think that in particular for those of us who

have come out of spiritual communities where grace was rarely, if ever, shown and faith was fueled by rule-keeping, the freedom to give and receive grace is stunted, if not altogether deficient.

But what if our obedience to God is a response?

What if our understanding of grace and the gospel informs how we behave? What if, when we fail, as we do (and often), we know because the Bible tells us so, that He will never leave us or forsake us? And what if we give that same grace to others?

Don't be tempted to throw the baby out with its proverbial bathwater. Giving grace, forgiveness, mercy, and understanding to a fellow sinner doesn't automatically cross out the consequences of choices, sin, and action. There is a right and proper place for church discipline, but ranking people on a netherworld spiritual scale must not be allowed to lodge there.

Now, turn back and apply all of what you just read to yourself.

Often, we can give grace to others but we cannot give grace to ourselves. What does it look like to accept God's grace for ourselves?

I mean, if we show unmerited grace to ourselves, suddenly we've opened up Pandora's Box, right?

If we give grace to ourselves, then we will just do what we want, and we can't have that!

But what if our obedience to God is a response?

What if our understanding of grace and the gospel informs how we behave? What if, when we fail, as we do (and often), we know because the Bible tells us so, that He will never leave us or forsake us? And what if we give that same grace to ourselves?

Don't be tempted to throw the baby out with its proverbial bathwater. Giving grace, forgiveness, mercy, and understanding to our ourselves doesn't automatically cross out the consequences of our choices, sin, and action. There is a right and proper place for church discipline, but ranking ourselves on a netherworld spiritual scale must not be allowed to lodge there.

Don't live there. Instead, live in the space where Christ dwells, learning to live as the loved and treasured child of God that you are.

When Satan tempts me to despair,

And tells me of the guilt within,

Upward I look, and see Him there

Who made an end of all my sin. (1)

"Who made an end of all my sin."

Moving forward looks like this: forgiveness of others, forgiveness of ourselves. Grace for others, grace for ourselves. Love for God, love for others, love for ourselves.

Moving forward out of a legalistic lifestyle might not be without pain and struggle, and the path will most certainly be laden with bumps and pitfalls, but there will also be victories and plenty of holes-in-one. Because God made an end to all of your sin, there isn't anything you can do to make it any less so. The bumps, the pitfalls, the victories, the holes-in-one—they will be there regardless of our sin. Better yet, they will be accompanied by the God who loves us and who pursues us into the deepest, darkest places until we are restored fully to and with him in eternity.

Until then, rest in the knowledge that He will heal and restore. And in regards to the crushing community and religious behavior you are taking steps away from: Simply breathe in, breathe out, and move on.

Questions to Ask Yourself

1. Much in the same way that we can struggle with believing God's unearned love for us, we can struggle with giving ourselves grace. List several ways in which you have not given yourself grace to be less than perfect while caught up in legalism.

2. List several ways in which you have not given yourself grace to be less than perfect as you have left your legalistic community.

3. Is there someone you need to apologize to? Are you willing to run into the burning building for the sake of loving God and loving others? For the sake of relationship?

4. What does it look like for you to "breathe in"? (Example: Reminding ourselves daily of the simple gospel.)

5. What does it look like for you to "breathe out"? (Example: Taking captive all of your thoughts about past conversations, people from your former church still judging you, and harbored hurts, and giving them over to God.)

6. What will it take for you to "move on"? List the practical ways in which you need to leave the past behind. List the spiritual ways in which you need to move on.

Resources For More Healing Ahead

Join a community of recovering legalists on Facebook. You are not alone!

www.facebook.com/groups/leavinglegalism/

More words of grace and encouragement, with a giant dose of the gospel every time I write here:

www.kendrafletcher.com

Acknowledgements

Every day I am just taken aback as I face the grace of God. Who knew he'd give me words to write and a passion to see them read for the sake of the gospel—for the sake of seeing other recovering legalists free from the bondage of our own hope-shifting? He gets all the glory.

I am thankful for a husband who has walked each step with me since 1989, back when we were carefree college students who knew it all. I'm also pretty speechless when I think of all he's put up with being married to me, but then, somehow I find new words with which to overwhelm him when he comes home from work at the end of the day.

So very thankful for the encouragement of some key people who read *Leaving Legalism* and gave me their valuable feedback:

Jim Applegate
Marcy Crabtree
Kimm Crandall

KENDRA FLETCHER | 105

Robin Demurga
Kristi Gregg
Matt Johnson
Tray and Melody Lovvorn
Tricia Otto
Dawn Terzo
Hal & Melanie Young

I have the best, most encouraging readers, and for each of you who cheered me on and kept telling me to keep going because you needed to read this book, I am grateful. Sometimes writing feels very lonely and all you see from the vantage point of your laptop is how well everyone else seems to be doing it. Thank you for reminding me that God had a job for me to do.

KENDRA FLETCHER

About the Author

Kendra Fletcher is a mother of 8, speaker, author, and podcaster. She is the author of *Lost and Found: Losing Religion, Finding Grace* and she regularly writes for Key Life Ministries. The Fletchers reside in California, where they play in the Pacific Ocean as often as possible.

Where she writes:
www.kendrafletcher.com

Faith can seem easy when
everything is going right...
What about when everything isn't?

This is a book that just might
change your life!
Steve Brown

Kendra Fletcher reveals the
beauty and grace of God
found in the midst of real pain
in honest people.
Jim Applegate

...see the wonderful
freedom that comes from
being lost and found...
Elyse M. Fitzpatrick

The message Kendra has
to share is one that can
only be described as
desperately needed.
Durenda Wilson

For anyone who has a
fresh encounter with
their own story."
Barrett Johnson

...will identify with Kendra
...who admits to faults and
still moves with her as she
finds her identity in Christ.
Jessica Thompson

Compelling, compassionate
Sally Clarkson

A truly gospel-centered,
Christ-exalting read.
Kimm Crandall

This book isn't pages. It's a compass that points you
toward the Light, toward Christ, toward a life liberated to
be freely and completely who you are in Christ.
Ann Voskamp

Lost & Found
Losing Religion, Finding Grace

Read the compelling story of how the Fletchers
found their world turned upside down as they
nearly lost three children in the span of 18
months.

New Growth Press * Barnes and Noble
Christian Book Distributors * Amazon